click!

To Jen,
Have fun!
Annabel Monaghan
&
Elisabeth Wolfe

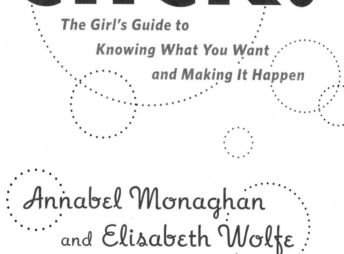

click!

The Girl's Guide to
Knowing What You Want
and Making It Happen

Annabel Monaghan
and Elisabeth Wolfe

Simon Pulse
New York London Toronto Sydney

SIMON PULSE

An imprint of Simon & Schuster Children's Publishing Division

1230 Avenue of the Americas, New York, NY 10020

Copyright © 2007 by Annabel Monaghan and Elisabeth Wolfe

All rights reserved, including the right of reproduction in whole
or in part in any form.

SIMON PULSE and colophon are registered trademarks of
Simon & Schuster, Inc.

Designed by Joel Avirom and Jason Snyder

The text of this book was set in Whitney.

Manufactured in the United States of America

First Simon Pulse edition November 2007

10 9 8 7 6 5 4 3 2 1

Library of Congress Control Number 2007932779

ISBN-13: 978-1-4169-5790-4

ISBN-10: 1-4169-5790-1

For Natalie Wilson, who makes things happen.

—A. S. M.

*For my soul mate, Ed. Thank you for helping
to make me happen.*

—E. K. W.

contents

(Hope We're Not Too) Foreword

Do you ever wonder why it's "happening" for some people but maybe not "happening" so much for you? Have you ever felt like you're walking through life feeling a little bit like Homer Simpson, stuck in a series of perpetual "D'ohs!"? If you feel like life has been making you happen, and not the other way around, this book just may be for you.

We wrote this book because we thought you might want to know what's up. As we get older, every year we learn a little something new about how the world works. We hear it from people we meet, our parents tell us things they never told us before, or a new study comes out. It's like some big society of elders is trickling information to us slowly, as we earn it. And with each new piece of information we want to shout, *Why didn't I know this when I was trying to get guys to like me by calling them six times a day?!*

Like a good friend with some helpful 411, we'd like to tell you what you need to know when you need to know it. We don't have all the answers, but what we can pass along might be just enough to get you thinking in a slightly different way. Are you ready? Let's change the rules and amend the bylaws to lower the age of initiation. As of right now, you're in. You are our first pledge class. Welcome!

introduction

Annabel's Story

When I was fifteen years old I was madly in love with Sam Denton.
I could describe in excruciating detail what his shoulders looked like
when he got out of the ocean. He was smart, he was hot, he was
popular. He was "it." I'd seen him every day that summer at the beach,
and then in the fall at parties. He definitely knew my name, but every
time I saw him around the "punch bowl" (names of beverages have
been changed to protect my parents), I'd lose my capacity for speech.
In short, Sam Denton thought I was a geek.

I thought about him all the time. I was truly lovesick and did
not know what to do to get him to like me. I obsessed over why he
didn't like me. I complained to my parents that my clothes weren't
right, I complained to my friends that my body wasn't right, and
I complained to myself that, well, *I* just wasn't right. I was really
starting to hate being me because being me wasn't getting me any
closer to being with Sam Denton.

Poor me. I called my sister who was away at college and poured out my heart. What my sister told me was this: Figure out what you want, write it down, and it will be yours. "What do you want?" she asked. "Sam Denton, duh," I said. "More specific!" she commanded. "I want Sam Denton to ask me to the prom!" I said. "When do you want it? When you're thirty? The universe needs to know, be specific," she went on. "I want Sam Denton to ask me to the prom on April 12," I said. "Write that down and tape it by your bed. Consider it done."

Clearly my sister had gone around the bend, but I was desperate. So I took a sheet of computer paper and wrote "Sam Denton will ask me to the prom on April 12." I taped it to the wall next to my bed and saw it every morning when I woke up and every night when I went to sleep. It stayed there for three months and became part of the mess that surrounded it. In a way Sam became a part of my surroundings and the idea of him became sort of familiar to me. I'd drift off to sleep thinking about what it would be like to go to the prom with him. I'd imagine what I'd wear and what music we'd dance to and what we'd look like together. This became sort of a fun going-to-sleep ritual for me.

In the weeks that followed, life got busy. Sam Denton was still "it," but the student council elections were in full swing, and I'd won for junior class president. My days became less about drooling over Sam and more about organizing fund-raisers, passing my classes, and catching up with my friends. Although I was psyched to bump into Sam at the beach, I no longer raced off to the girls' room to completely overhaul my hair and makeup beforehand. One day when

Sam asked to borrow my sunscreen, I found myself answering him coherently, without breaking into a cold sweat. Sophomore year was agreeing with me.

So here's the punchline: On April 12, I was at the supermarket with my mom. I was stuffing Granny Smith apples into a bag when Sam walked into the produce department. "Hi," he said. I think I said hi back. He went on, "I've been wanting to call you but I didn't have your number. Are you going to the spring prom?" The rest of the story is a lot like you'd expect: a stammering yes, an awkward number exchange, my mom pretending to study the avocados, and a fun prom.

What Happened?

Why did this work for Annabel? Is it magic? Did taping a piece of paper really bring poor, unsuspecting Sam Denton into her life? Not really. The principle at work here is that thoughts have energy. When you take the focus off what is missing in your life and put it on what you want, your energy shifts. When you are putting out positive, unwavering energy, your world begins to change before your eyes.

But there's a lot more to wanting and getting than meets the eye. There's also figuring out what you want and why you want it, and then feeling good enough to really make it happen. This is hard work. You will face challenges and setbacks, but the path to making it happen is what strengthens your desire and tests your inner resolve. It makes you get in touch with not only who you are, but who you are capable of being.

Once you begin to make "it" happen, your confidence in your ability to achieve will grow and you will be able to pick a new goal and do it again and again. This book is designed to give you the information and practical tools you need to start putting out more positive energy.

We'll begin with a general introduction to the concept of energy, how to make it work for you, and how to apply it to all the other stuff you have going on. At the end of the book, you'll find a four-week journal that includes a day planner to help you manage all the things you have to do and create better energy around all the things you want to do.

how the universe works:
let's get started

how energy works

We Are Energy

Have you ever met somebody for barely a second and decided that you liked them? What was it about them? Most likely it was their energy. You probably say things all the time like, "He puts out a bad vibe" or "There's just something about her . . ." You are talking about their energy. We all have it in us, around us, and shooting out of our every pore at every moment. People's energy reflects their deeply held beliefs. You can spot "Everyone's out to get me" just as easily as "I've got it all going on" from across a room.

Have you ever walked into a party painfully aware that your underwear is too tight and that you have a huge, underground zit on your chin? Neither of these conditions is evident to anyone but you, but your uncomfortable energy tells everyone in the room that something's up. If anyone talked to you at all, it was probably to ask if you were okay. Your energy was vibrating on the opposite of fun: awkward.

Everything Is Energy

It's not just you. Everything around you is energy. And although you may not realize it, the chair you are sitting on right now, while it seems solid, is actually vibrating energy. Same goes for your computer, cell phone, iPod, and even your dog. Albert Einstein was onto something with $E=mc^2$. Essentially everything is energy . . . moving, vibrating, ever changing energy.

You have thousands of thoughts every day. And if you think something long enough, it becomes a belief. Every belief you have is a form of vibrating energy that you can perceive.

Try this: Look in the mirror and try to keep your face still. Call to mind the most amazing thought you can. Are you at a fitting for the dress that Armani himself has designed for your trip down the red carpet on your big night, when you will accept the Oscar for your brilliant portrayal of Audrey Hepburn? Okay, that was ours. Now think of the worst scenario you can. Notice how without changing your expression, you look totally different. This is your perception of your energy.

Try this: Take your pointer fingers and your thumbs and put them together to make two "okay" signs. Now link the two circles, so it looks like the Master Card logo. Think something true like "My name is . . ." and try to pull your circles apart. Now think something you know not to be true like "There's nothing more appealing than a juicy zit." Now pull your circles apart. What was the difference? You probably noticed that the true thought made your muscles stronger.

We're Not Making This Stuff Up

First of all, let us take off our lab coats for a second and introduce ourselves. We are not scientists, psychologists, or palm readers. We're just two people who do a lot of positive thinking. And we have seen amazing changes in our lives as a result of shifting our beliefs to reflect the energy of what we want. We are experts at nothing except what we've seen in our own lives and what we've observed in the lives of those who have shared their stories with us. We want you to see these kinds of changes in your life too. You could probably sum up the crux of our philosophy on our favorite bumper sticker: *Wag more, bark less.*

There's a crowd of scientists, psychologists, quantum physicists, kinesiologists, and monks who could explain the energy principles at work in excruciating detail. We'd like to save you a little time, so here it is in a nutshell.

You've probably heard in biology class that neurons in our brains act like electrical cables, transmitting measurable electrical impulses or messages at high speeds between the brain, the spinal cord, and the body. Bored already? Stay with us.

Scientists have not only demonstrated that thoughts have energy but that this "thought energy" can be transmitted out to the world. In 1966, Cleve Backster, one of the most well respected lie detector examiners in the United States, attached lie detector electrodes to the leaf of a plant to see what it would do. Knowing that lie detector readings change when humans are under stress, he decided to see if he could elicit a stress response in the plant. First he watered the plant and found no meaningful change in the lie detector reading. Then he actually dipped the plant's leaves in hot coffee . . . still no change in the reading. However, when he contemplated getting matches to burn the plant, the polygraph moved wildly. It was as if his violent thoughts were felt by the plant.

More recently, another scientist, Masaru Emoto, found that merely attaching positive words like "THANK YOU" to a bottle of water and freezing it formed beautiful hexagonal crystals. When the same experiment was conducted with the negative word "FOOL," the water formed crystals that were broken and misshapened. The water actually responded to the energy of the word that was attached to the bottle. The study showed that words—whether they be thought, spoken, or written—all have energy. The vibration from positive words benefits our world, but the vibration from negative words can be really harmful.

Another ongoing study called the Global Consciousness Project has shown that when masses of people concentrate on a single incident like a sporting event, the Academy Awards, a natural disaster, or a terrorist attack (such as those that occurred September 11), the measurable energy emitted from those groups becomes orderly, rather than random. It is as if everyone's energy is focused on the same thing, resonates at the same frequency, and organizes itself.

The impact of energy on health has long been accepted in Eastern medicine. Energy is now being researched and used for healing in some of the most prestigious Western hospitals around the world from the Integrative Medicine Department at Memorial

Sloan-Kettering Cancer Center in New York City to Duke University Medical Center in Durham, North Carolina.

We could bore you about all this for another hundred pages, but boring you is not really what this book is about. Think of it as science, think of it as magic, or think of it as something else—whatever feels right to you. But it is undeniable that throughout the world, there is a groundswell of new interest in the connection between thoughts and energy. So if the idea of thoughts having energy feels like a big leap for you, stay tuned. Science is quickly building on this work, and it will be fascinating to see what new findings arise.

Vibes Matter

What do these studies have to do with you? A lot. Your thoughts matter. Think of the impact that you could have on your surroundings if you just think a little more positively. When you are feeling confident, you are putting one type of energy out (like when you wear your favorite jeans), and when you are feeling insecure you are putting another type of energy vibration (like when you had the underground monster zit). Each thought has its own unique energy vibration and those energy vibrations are shouting out to the world. If your beliefs about yourself help you to radiate love and self-confidence, you are a positive energy powerhouse. That's where we want you to be energetically. All the time.

Energy is not something you can go out and get. Your energy

comes from inside of you. You were born completely empowered, having everything that you need to live a blissful life. What we want you to do is turn up the volume on your joyful energy and then blow out the speakers with your confidence. Believing in yourself and feeling confident that you can achieve your goals will send out the energy to help make things happen. It is time to get back in touch with this power.

What Goes Around Comes Around

We agree with Justin Timberlake on that one—that's how we think life works. Life tends to be circular rather than linear. The earth is round and revolves around the sun. We are born needing to be protected and taken care of and eventually we grow old and revert in many ways back to childhood. We breathe in oxygen created by the trees and plants around us and exhale carbon dioxide required by the trees and plants to live. We are all connected; collectively, all people together represent humanity. Therefore it should not be surprising that your energy affects the energy of the people, animals, plants, and earth around you.

In this way your beliefs are constantly defining your experience. Your beliefs have energy that goes out and brings back things and experiences that vibrate in the same way. So what we are putting out into the world at any moment is what we're attracting back. Good vibes out . . . good things back. Bad vibes out . . . icky things back. You send it, you get it back. Remember when Wile E. Coyote threw the boomerang at the Roadrunner and it came right back and hit him in the head? Your beliefs are like that boomerang, and their energy will come right back to you. Every time. So don't end up at the bottom of the canyon.

Your energy is doing this during your every waking moment, constantly attracting things, events, and people to you that are a vibrational match with your energy. The quality of that energy (good or bad, positive or negative, Yippee! or Ugh!) determines what surrounds you. So whatever frequency goes out automatically attracts a similar frequency, causing things to happen in your life . . . good and bad, based on their matching vibrations.

Have you ever been thinking about your long-lost friend from two summers ago, remembering how hard you laughed trying to paddle your canoe, and all of a sudden your cell phone is ringing with that very person on the line? "OMG! I was just thinking about you!" It happens all the time, and that is the most basic example of your thoughts having energy and attracting that experience to you. Your energy said: I really want to talk to Ashley. And there she was.

Think of the last time you walked into a party feeling excited about how much fun you were going to have. You looked forward to it all week, imagined how it would be, and walked in already feeling the music and having a good time. You probably found that fun surrounded you immediately. You were vibrating the energy of fun before you even got there, and when you opened the door, there it was.

Or how about the time that everyone was talking about how hard the geometry test was going to be. You are usually pretty good at geometry but all the talk about the monster test psyched you out. By the time the test rolled around, your hands were so sweaty that you couldn't hold your protractor and compass. Suddenly, none of the questions made any sense to you at all. You weren't as shocked as your teacher was when you completely flunked.

What about the new comedy that's supposed to be so funny? You've seen the trailer, you've seen the commercials, and all your friends are talking about it. It is supposed to be the funniest movie ever. As you buy your ticket, you're already starting to giggle in anticipation. By the time the lights go out in the theater you find yourself laughing at the talking popcorn bag who's reminding you to throw away your trash. The movie may be actually be funny on its own, but it doesn't matter because you have set yourself up to literally drag the funny out of it to meet the "funny" energy you're putting out.

You've probably heard that you are what you eat. The truth is you are what you believe. Everything around you is a result of the energy your thoughts and beliefs are putting out. No matter how busy you think you are, you are probably even busier than that. It's as if your energy is working hard at every moment creating and writing the script for your life. The million dollar question is, *What are you writing?*

Focus Factor

Where are your thoughts? What are you focusing on? The Focus Factor says this: You get what you focus on. By focusing on something and believing in it deep down to your core, your energy actually starts vibrating at its frequency. The problem is that most people spend their time focusing on the things they don't want. And usually if you think you want something really badly, you are more focused on the fact that you don't have it. That's the first habit we want to break.

For example, maybe you're thinking: *I want a boy to like me.* (Or a girl, whatever floats your boat.) Your thoughts should be as straightforward as, *I want a boy to like me, I focus on the idea, take the right steps, and voilà . . . I have him.* But chances are your focus looks more like this: *I want a boyfriend. I am so lonely and it seems like everyone else is paired up. No guys talk to me at parties and I end up being the only one not hooked up at the end of the night.* So, why don't you have the object of your desire? Anyone? Because you are completely focused on feeling lonely. You are more focused on what you *don't* have than on what you *do* want. And the Focus Factor promises that you attract what you focus on most intensely.

Instead, focus on what it would feel like to have a boyfriend. Would you go to the party together or just meet there with your friends? What would it feel like to get there and know there was a guy who was into you? Would you talk on the phone at night or just IM while you're doing your homework? Can you smell the coconut suntan lotion on his skin after a day at the beach? Can you feel good imagining it? If it brings you happiness to imagine it, then it is likely that more of that kind of happiness is on its way.

Or let's say you've had a particularly grueling finals week. You've barely slept, your body aches from hunching over your desk. All you want is to get away, rest, and have a good time. Great news! Your parents just announced that they're taking you to the beach for the week. If you think: *At last! This is exactly what I needed* (so far, so good), *but I just hope I don't have to share a room with my little brother. He is so disgusting! And my parents are going to be at the beach in their totally embarrassing bathing suits saying, "Go talk to those boys, honey, they look nice,"* your vacation probably will be a bust. Instead, try to focus here: *It is going to be so great to be at the beach with nothing to do. I can feel the sand between my toes and the sun on my skin. I have been dying to start the sequel to that novel I read last time we went away. My parents do take us out for nice dinners.* Focus on a relaxing beach week and you'll probably get just that. Just don't forget *Gossip Girl*!

Focus on making the tennis team, you probably will, provided you also happen to practice and show up for tryouts. Focus on the fact that you didn't make it last year and that the whole process is unfair and the girls on the tennis team have so much fun and you are never a part of it . . . that's what you'll get. Your focus is on *not* being on the tennis team. We could do this all day.

Take a minute and think about Cady in *Mean Girls*. (Haven't seen it? Well, welcome to the planet Earth. We hope you come in peace. Now go to Netflix.com and rent it.) She tells us that since she has started her vendetta against Regina George (the most popular girl in school), she spends 80 percent of her time talking about her and 20 percent of her time trying to get other people to talk about her. Cady is beyond focused—let's call it obsessed—with trying to ruin Regina. And by focusing in this way, she is of course not focusing on what she wants, which is for Aaron (the cute boy) to like her. Instead, her focus is on the fact that Regina George is a bitch. Everything escalates, Regina hits an all-time fever pitch of bitchiness, and Cady loses her friends and the respect of her teacher. In short, Cady got more of what she focused on and none of what she wanted. By focusing on destroying Regina's life, she destroyed her own. It wasn't until Cady released her death grip on Regina and started to be herself that Aaron really started to like her.

As a nod to Hollywood, we admit that *Mean Girls* would have been a serious bore if Cady had read this book. She would have stayed true to herself (didn't she even look better before she went mental over Regina?), not faked dumb in math, and would have ended up the coolest girl in school as the Hot Smart Exotic Girl from Africa. She would have ended up kissing Aaron at the end of the movie anyway, but the movie would have lasted about twelve minutes. Loved all the drama, but let's leave it on the silver screen and focus on what we want for ourselves, in our lives.

The Focus Factor can cause a snowball effect. Watch how the Focus Factor can make a typical morning snowball into either a disaster of a day, or one of the best days of your life:

Consider this day: *You wake up on the right side of the bed. Your coffee tastes great, your jeans zip, your hair cooperates. You are two minutes early for school, that cute guy from the football team is reassigned to your history class. Your English teacher loved your paper, the recruiter from your dream college happens to strike up a conversation with you in line at Starbucks. Your parents are planning a trip out of town. It doesn't end.*

Consider this day: *Everything's the same but you slept too late to get your math homework finished before school. Then you miss your ride. You walk to school instead and the most annoying person in the world decides to walk along with you and ask you a thousand questions. You get to school late to find out that that same person has been reassigned to your history class. You bump into some old guy on the way into Starbucks, cut in front of him in line, and find out he's the recruiter for your dream college. Same day, different energy.*

So what's the difference? On the good day you felt good, your energy was positive, you loved your coffee, and that good feeling brought more things to feel good and grateful about. If you look at your life with an *Aren't I Lucky?* attitude, more great "luck" will come to you. When your focus is positive, life feels great. On the bad day, you started out grousing and blaming and fretting. You focused all day on the things that were going wrong and attracted more of them into your experience. The snowball effect works for good things and bad things. We are going to show you how to get more of a handle on this process, so that you can recognize when it's happening. Then maybe you can laugh about it and refocus on what you want.

Isn't it funny how you can go six months or more sometimes without boys paying attention to you, then you go on one date, start feeling more positive, and suddenly two other guys start texting you? It seems like when it rains . . . it pours.

Before we go any further, we'd like to make one more point about the Focus Factor. We have said that the Universe will deliver to you more of what you focus on, but not everything in your life has been brought on by your focus. If you have been reading this thinking, *OMG! This summer my parents got divorced, and I broke my leg when a careless driver rear-ended me the week before swim team tryouts. Is it all my fault? Did I do that to myself?* The answer is no. There are some things in your life that happen because of other people or because, inexplicably, they have to happen for a reason you may never know. We want you to look at what you are focused on now and understand that if you whine about your totally unfair principal 24/7, there will be more to whine about. So please don't get into blaming yourself for the myriad other things that happen that are beyond your control. All you can control about those less-than-desirable situations is how you react to them moving forward. This book really is about just that, moving forward.

e-vites

The Law of E-vitation

Let's take the Focus Factor into the twenty-first century. You know what an E-vite is, right? What a brilliant way to instantaneously invite exactly who you want to a party. With just a little bit of pre-planning, you can go online, choose a theme, pick a design, fill in the "who/what/where" of your party, create your guest list, and maybe even write something corny like "Just Bring Yourselves." Then click send and it goes out over some unimaginably complex network and arrives precisely where you want it to. You just kick back and wait for your RSVPs to roll in.

We like to think of energy in the same way: At its essence, sending out your energy is like sending a constant stream of E-vites to the Universe. There's just one catch: The Universe's RSVP is always yes. (Remember the boomerang?) So stop and think before you click send.

Let's say you are sending out energy that reads like this E-vite: *Let's get this party started! Join me for the most exciting and amazing life ever!* The Universe will RSVP yes, and will be there ready to rock with you. Don't send out an E-vite that reads: *It's time for the most miserable life ever!* The Universe will RSVP yes, and will be there with bells on, waiting to provide you with all the "guests" you need to create all the mishaps and disasters you are dreading.

The Universe can be relied upon to say yes to your E-vite every single time. Knowing this, don't be careless about what you are asking for. Channel your inner P-Diddy, and make sure your party is THE party. You don't want stale potato chips, flat cola, and day-old cake, do you? Keep it strictly A-list and be careful about the energy you are sending out.

E-vite Composition 101

It's a funny world we live in. Listen to your friends talk at lunch and what you'll mostly hear is the chant of the two evil stepsisters: Bitching and Moaning. Ditto at your family gatherings, and even online at Facebook. Next time you are waiting on line at the drug store, listen in to how much people are complaining to each other about something. When you imagine the E-vites flowing out of them, it's actually kind of amusing.

In this culture, focusing on what we don't want is just what we like to do. We'll be the first ones to admit that sometimes it feels really good to bitch about what we don't have. The problem is that when we complain too much, what we are really doing is attracting more of what we don't want into our lives. We like to call it playing the V-card. No, not that V-card! This V-card isn't about losing anything but your power: By playing the victim, you actually become one. What you are really doing is clicking send on loss of control. Here is what we heard from two girls within seven minutes in line at the local pizza place.

COMPLAINT	E-VITE SENT	RSVP
My day is ruined! I can't believe Mrs. Jones embarrassed me like that in art.	*I am a victim of humiliation.*	*Yes*
I am never going to be elected to the student council. I lost last year and no one takes me seriously.	*I am a victim of public opinion.*	*Yes*
There is not enough time to do everything I need to do.	*I am a victim of the space-time continuum.*	*Yes*
There are not enough cute guys at our school and the only normal ones are taken.	*I am a victim of the laws of supply and demand.*	*Yes*

Take a second to think about your top five most recently played complaints. What is the focus of each complaint? That's the E-vite you are sending. Are you playing the V-card? If so, what are you a victim of? Notice how every complaint gets you a step closer to feeling like a victim.

We know these thoughts aren't pretty, but you can turn them around by rewriting them. If you don't feel like turning them around—no problem. You can always join the thousands of people around you who have enlisted in the Army of Complainers. You've met them for sure. Nothing goes their way; everyone else has more than they do; their Frappuccino's not cold; someone's just ruined their life by selling the last cinnamon raisin bagel. It's really nothing more than a habit, and why wouldn't it be? Complaining brings more stuff to complain about and the next thing you know you're up to three packs of Unfiltered Boo Hoos a day.

To Click or Not to Click

It's not like every thought you have forms into an E-vite that's sent out to the Universe. It's your collective thoughts—the ones you focus on the most and which form your mood—that compose your E-vites. In any situation you have, with practice, the choice is whether or not to click send on the E-vite you've written. Let's say you want to be chosen as editor of the school newspaper. It has been your dream to have this position since the first day you walked into the newspaper office. You have done everything possible from updating your resume and collecting your clips to wearing a newsboy hat and stalking the current editor to make this happen. You've clicked send on that: *Great job!*

Then two weeks before they are going to announce the new editor, you find out that Melissa Parker, aka Smartest, Most Perfect Girl Ever, has decided that she wants to try for it too. You may feel a barrage of negative thoughts coming to you: *Oh no . . . this totally sucks! I'll never get it now!* But as you feel your emotions starting to snowball, take a deep breath and try to stop the emotionally charged thoughts from gaining too much momentum. If you can feel your way back to a place of confidence and happiness over getting the job, you'll be back to clicking send on: *I will be the editor.*

Let's say you don't get a hold of yourself and keep going on and on about this. You start envisioning how awful it will feel to have to look at the name Melissa Parker on the masthead of the school newspaper for an entire year. You go on in this way thinking: *I can't believe this! It was my dream, not hers, and this always happens to me! I can't stand her. Why does she get everything and I get nothing?!* Guess what? You just clicked send on an E-vite that read *Come to a Pity Party in honor of me.* You remember what the RSVP is, right? *Yes.*

In other words, you unconsciously click send when you get all worked up about something and focus on it too long. That's when you can get stuck in traffic between two places we like to call Blamingham and Victimville. We want you to stop at that point where you are about to attach a chain of strong emotion to something you don't want. It would be smooth sailing if you could figure out how to follow your *Oh no . . . this sucks!* with *But that's okay. I have much more newspaper experience than she has. It doesn't make sense that she'd be chosen just because she has such good grades. Managing a paper is a lot more than that, and I have what it takes.* Okay, we feel better, do you? You calmed down, brought yourself to a better emotional state, and then clicked send on: *I am capable, I deserve this.* RSVP: *Yes.* You are no victim.

What If It's Too Late?

The good news is that it's never too late. All it takes is a second to hit cancel, rewrite your E-vite, and summon up better emotions to send it on its way. It's your E-vite and you can cancel the party anytime you want. It's just easier to do before the party has gotten into full swing and the neighbors have already called the cops. Maybe you've been sending out negative energy for a while and are just realizing it now. Well, just quickly hit cancel and rewrite those old E-vites.

The truth is that sometimes you are going to totally lose it and get your panties in a wad. It's one of the things that separates human beings from robots and it's not likely to change. It's often impossible to immediately get hold of your emotions and take a step back. The important thing here is that if you realize that you are in a situation that is composing an intricate E-vite to disaster and doom, slow down and don't let yourself click send!

When something unexpected and hideous happens, notice the thought that comes to you and feel the emotion behind it. But take a second afterward to decide how much power you are going to give the mishap. Are you going to let a broken nail snowball into a broken heart? Your challenge is to try to find a way to feel better quickly so that what you are sending out will bring about better circumstances.

Let's go back to that good day–bad day example. So you wake up in the morning, your coffee tastes great, and then you spill it all over your new white jeans. Make a choice. Is this going to be the beginning of a downward spiral that will end in an afternoon fender bender? Or can you nip it in the bud? *Oh no. This totally sucks! But I do have another pair of jeans in my drawer to wear. These white jeans do look better when they are fresh out of the dryer. I'll wear them tomorrow and they'll look even better. I wonder if that new red sweater will look good with my other jeans. . . .* If you can get there, click send. E-vite reads *It's all good.* The RSVP, *Yes. It is.*

One Click at a Time

You are probably starting to panic over all the negative E-vites you've already sent. How were you supposed to know that your energy was like a stream of E-vites going out to the Universe? No worries, you can always start over. If you've been dwelling for the past few days on the fear of freezing up while giving your speech on Friday, you may have already sent an E-vite. That's okay. You can cancel that *Fear Factor* cast party, plus you have the rest of the week to rewrite your E-vite: *Hey, just because I forgot my lines in the sixth-grade play doesn't mean that I can't speak in public. . . . This isn't sixth grade, I'm so different now. It's not just me, everyone gets a little nervous before speaking in public.* That E-vite reads *I'm going to do great!* Keep your focus there—you have all week!—and that will be your dominant E-vite.

But what if you don't have all week? What if the speech is in twenty minutes? Don't worry about that either. The strength of your E-vite lies more in the intensity of your feeling and the depth of your belief that you can make a great speech than in the amount of time you've been clicking send. Take the time you have to really imagine yourself as articulate and poised, feel yourself giving the speech and believe that you are capable. You'll be channeling your inner Oprah in no time.

Think of your energy like a pie graph that totals 100 percent. If you are feeling good and clicking send on positive E-vites, say, 51 percent of the time, then you're doing great. We are not suggesting that you master total mind control. In fact, the thought of it frightens us to death. But you can assume that if most of your beliefs are in line with what you want and you are feeling pretty good, you are inviting good things in. A little bit of self-doubt won't sabotage you.

Start slow. Even if you can be clicking send on more positive E-vites 1 percent more than you are now, you are moving in the right direction. A 51 percent in algebra would be a big fat F in school, but in this book it is more than enough to get you where you want to go. (Don't you wish we were your teachers?)

The RSVP—Managing Your Inbox

Your inbox is full of the yes RSVPs to your E-vites. Have you heard the expression "Be careful what you wish for, because you just might get it"? That probably applies best here. Sometimes you check your inbox and the RSVP is just what you asked for and it wasn't quite as great as you'd imagined. What if you bought yourself an awesome vintage shirt on eBay, but as you opened the box you are hit with a flurry of moths and a waft of the previous owner's BO? Would you still wear it? You ordered it and it came, but you can still send it back and order something else.

A lot of times when you are looking in your inbox, you don't recognize your RSVP because it is in a slightly different package than you'd imagined. So let's say you are obsessed with Pete Wentz from Fall Out Boy. You focus on him all the time, the thought of him gets you all emotionally charged. Hello? Where's your RSVP? He should be knocking on your door as we speak. Right?

Not quite. The most important part of any want is the "why," so we are going to have to ask the question here. You've never actually met this guy, so we can't say for sure that you're soul mates. What is real is your intention and how you feel. If you take a second and ask yourself WHY you are so into this guy, you might find that what you like is what you think he is. You want a guy who appreciates good music and is kind and fun to be around. Focus on those qualities and how they make you feel. You'll probably find yourself feeling more creative, kind, and fun. If that's not enough, go check your inbox—a different guy with those qualities is probably waiting.

If you double-check the cover of this book, you'll notice that it's not by Annabel *Denton* and Elisabeth Wolfe. Annabel did go to the prom with Sam, but he didn't turn out to be the love of her life. Instead she met another guy, and then another guy after that, until she met the guy that was perfect for her, the one that she had been E-viting her whole life. Look at all the stuff the Universe is giving you with excited anticipation, knowing that the best thing is on its way.

As your life unfolds before you, it becomes sadly apparent that the Universe is actually smarter than you are. Once you decide what you want, it's easy to get a little hyper-focused on it. Let's say you've applied for a World Teach summer program where you are going to be teaching English to children in a small village in Costa Rica. You feel so excited about it and you think about what an adventure it will be to be so far from home, how amazing it will be to live in such a different culture, what it will feel like to make a difference. You have focused on it, you feel great about it. Your E-vite reads *Amazing cultural experience*. But when the decision day comes, you race to the mailbox and find a letter that says, "We are sorry to inform you that we will not be able to offer you a position . . ." You are crushed. You sulk. Why didn't it work? You wanted it so badly and you focused so well. Just hang tight, because . . .

Ring-a-ling-a-ling! Hello? What's that? You want me to come to the Himalayas for the summer to help stimulate their economy by importing local art into the United States? Harvard's sponsoring the program but they need one more girl? Even better—I love art! The RSVP always comes through, so be a little flexible.

Another Kind of E-vite, Or Plan B

If you are looking around you and see lots of things in your inbox that you wish you had never invited, you probably want to hit that handy delete button. And as much as we'd love to stretch the metaphor that far, it's not quite that simple. The closest you can get to a delete button is just refocusing and sending out new E-vites. Cady did it in *Mean Girls* when her inbox was full of RSVPs that read *Yes! Your Teacher Hates You, Yes! Your Friends Hate You,* and *Yes! This Has Blown Up in Your Face.* She could have dwelled there and kept clicking send but, instead, she moved on. She started composing new E-vites focusing on what she wanted. She won the math competition, and won her old friends back, as well as the heart of Aaron. As soon as you can start clicking send on something else—call it Plan B—the old RSVP that you didn't want will move down on your inbox list and won't matter so much.

Actress Jennifer Hudson could be the ultimate spokesperson for having a Plan B. Despite her amazing vocal range, Jennifer was booted off *American Idol* while less vocally talented performers remained. But Jennifer didn't put all her eggs in the *American Idol* basket and quickly moved on and focused on what she wanted: an acting career. The following year, she was cast in the role of Effie White in *Dreamgirls,* for which she won a Golden Globe and an Academy Award. E-vite: *Golden Globes afterparty.* RSVP: *Yes.* Now compare Jennifer's strategy to that of some of the other performers we see leave the show crying and complaining about Simon, never to be heard from again. Do they have a Plan B? What are they focusing on? E-vite: *Come to my Life's Not Fair Party.* RSVP: *Yes.*

Maybe you've learned firsthand how much easier life can be if you have a Plan B. Like the time you wanted to see the new romantic comedy that was sold out the minute you got to the front of the ticket line at the theater. That's okay. You saw the drama that had received rave reviews instead. Two thumbs-up for having a Plan B! Or maybe you went out to dinner and ordered the chicken wings. When the waiter came back and told you they're all out, did you fall apart, or order a cheeseburger? If you went for the next best thing, you sent this E-vite: *I can go with the flow.* RSVP: *Yes.*

In the journal at the back of this book there is a space to write down your Plan B and keep track of the steps you are taking to make sure it is available to you. Some of the hardest times people have are when they put all their eggs in one basket, and then they turn into a basket case when things don't work out exactly as they plan. Remember that it's a feeling you are going for, so having a Plan B gives the Universe a little wiggle room.

Archive Your Old Items Now

Let's face it, there's a lot of garbage in your head from the media, your parents, and your preschool teacher that you don't necessarily want or need in there. People have been sharing their thoughts (thanks for sharing!) until these thoughts have became so comfortable that they have unpacked their bags and moved onto your hard drive as full-blown beliefs. Some of these thoughts were positive ("She's the smart one") and others not so much ("Her sister's the pretty one"). Many of these beliefs are the essence of what you are currently clicking send on.

Think of all the negative stuff the media wants you to click send on. Call us crazy, but we find the newspapers and evening news more frightening than *The Ring.* Advertisements, magazines, and our culture of celebrity bombard us with what's hot and what's not. It's a wonder any of us dare to leave the house without a bulletproof vest and a pair of fake boobs.

It's probably not too hard to figure out which relatives, teachers, and friends specialized in nurturing your negative E-vites. You could dedicate a whole weekend to listing all your destructive beliefs and designing a flow chart to determine who's responsible for which. But the blame game is a wholly unsatisfying exercise. Who cares? Put down the V-card and let's move on.

Take a second to consider some of your thoughts that you don't really believe or want to believe anymore. Need help? How about "school's just not my thing" or "I'm totally lame at sports" or "nobody wants to hear what I have to say." Ask yourself why you believe things like "I suck at math" or "I am not a good student." Is it because of something your third grade teacher said? Would it make sense to rewrite that E-vite to read *When I focus on my homework, I actually do okay.* Or, *I am pretty good at word problems.* E-vite: *Capable.* RSVP: *Yes.*

What beliefs have you picked up from society? Without even being aware of it, were you under the impression that being a good friend meant putting yourself down and listening sympathetically while your friends bitched over a coffee? After all, that's what girls do on *Laguna Beach*, right?

You : *I am soooo fat.*

Friend: *No, I am soooo fat.*

You: *Oh, please. You are so skinny. OMG . . . did you see the size of this zit on my chin?*

Friend: *My skin is so much worse. I'd take acne over sun damage any day. Look at how much sun damage I have. See?*

Sound familiar? But now you've learned that talking about what's missing in our lives is just begging for more of the same. (Remember, E-vite: *Lack.* RSVP: *Yes*). Maybe now you'll begin to question your beliefs about what constitutes a healthy friendship.

We're not asking you to reformat your hard drive. That's a bit drastic and would overwrite all the great stuff you've picked up over the years. But what you can do is save over old files. Take any old belief you don't want to have anymore and turn it around. Write down the new belief, and use it as a bookmark so you see it all the time. Write it on your Facebook page (see page 55). Make that thought as familiar to you as that Verizon guy saying, "Can you hear me now?"

This book is about getting out of your own way so you can feel better about yourself and start attracting what you want into your life. Consciously compose your E-vites based on what you really believe (and want to believe!), and feel yourself getting closer to your goals.

tell me what you want, what you really, really want

TAKE IT FROM POSH AND THE SPICE GIRLS—take some time to tell yourself what you really, really want. As much time as you spend wanting stuff, sometimes it's really hard to choose exactly what you want. Some things are obvious to you that you want them. (We agree that it's more fun to go to a great concert than to babysit your aunt's cat.) Other things are trickier and all jumbled together. (Why exactly do you want to go out with the captain of the football team?)

Trying to determine exactly what you want is a very personal process. When you are doing it, try to listen to what's in your gut and listen only to the voice that you recognize as yours. Not your friends' voices, not your parents' voices. Your voice. It is impossible that you and all of your friends want the same things, the same guy, the same college, the same life. So as you work through this book, try this: Assume that everything that you say you want, you will really get. Your gut reaction will tell you if you really want it.

How to Figure Out What You Want

Have you ever gone to iTunes to download music for your iPod? There are lots of genres of music, hundreds of artists, and thousands of songs to choose from. How do you know which ones you want to download? You have the opportunity to design any playlist you want, to define your experience by selecting the soundtrack. Hmm, but what to download? This is exactly the process you go through when determining what you want.

Listening to song snippets/samples enables you to "test drive" the song without making a ninety-nine-cent commitment. Most of the time, you know within the first few seconds of listening to that snippet whether you'll purchase that song. You just know if the song does anything for you. You can't describe why exactly, but it sounds good.

Here's another example. It may seem silly, but think about the last time you washed your hands. You turned on the cold water, then turned on a little bit of hot. It still felt too cold, so you added more hot. When the water felt just right, you washed your hands. You knew instinctively what felt good.

Take this example. You order the double tall mocha latte that you've been dreaming about all morning from the greasy guy at the coffee shop. Just as he is about to secure the lid on it, he lets out a huge sneeze and snot flies everywhere. As he hands it to you, he says, "Thanks and have a nice day." Congratulations! You just figured out what you don't like.

Without much thought, we decide what we want and don't want on a daily basis. Our experiences force us to define what we want. Once we've determined our preferences, we intentionally choose more of what feels best. Think of life as one big iTunes, and you can download more of

how the universe works: let's get started

whatever experience feels good to you, and leave the stuff you don't like behind. Look at life as an opportunity to constantly create a new "playlist" of things you want. And as you sample new snippets (or life experiences), ask yourself if they feel good or bad to you. If they feel good to you, chances are you want more of them. So download them to your playlist.

→ *Here's your first exercise. Get out your pencil and write your playlist. What do you want with all your heart? Be specific.*

SEND		_ □ X
TO:	The Universe	
FROM:	Really Really Want It!	
CC:	The Whole World	
RE:	My Playlist	

Why Do You Want It?

Everything you want—from success in school to a better lip gloss—boils down to how you think it's going to make you feel. Will it make you feel happy? Confident? Loved? If you focus on those feelings, you are attracting more of them to you. When you focus on not having what you want, you may feel sad, insecure, or lonely. This is where it's easy to get stuck.

Based on what we now know about the energy of your thoughts and the Focus Factor, we suggest you make feeling happy your number-one goal. We hear your collective "duh." But when we asked girls, we were surprised that happiness wasn't one of the things they said they wanted. Instead, they claimed they wanted to be rich, more popular, have better clothes, have a better social life, more understanding parents, bigger boobs, smaller boobs, a better body, and higher grades. To "be happy" didn't even make the list.

But when we pressed girls to find out why they wanted these things, they said that they thought those things would make them happy. Achieving happiness was like the reward after a long, hard struggle.

The problem in this way of thinking is that the sorts of things you may want (despite what our cultural values may suggest) probably won't make you truly happy. Maybe a quick fix, but that's about all. You've probably seen this for yourself the last time you were dying for that new pair of pricey jeans you saved up for and finally bought. You felt the rush of taking them out of the shopping bag and out for a spin. But like any other buzz-inducing substance, the novelty wore off and you were onto the next.

Or maybe you thought that being part of the popular crowd would make you happy. You always envisioned hanging out with the cool people and getting invited to all the best parties. When you finally became friends with all the "right" people, it felt amazing at first. But after the initial buzz wore off, you didn't really feel that different. A little more confident maybe. But where was the happiness you craved?

The reality is that these things didn't actually bring you that feeling of happiness. It wasn't the jeans that gave you that quick feeling of happiness. It wasn't being popular that gave you the quick feeling of happiness. It was YOU that gave you the feeling of happiness. You just used the object of your desire to induce it. You had the ability to give it (a feeling) to yourself all along. Just like Dorothy in *The Wizard of Oz* didn't need the wizard to get back to Kansas, you don't need anything outside yourself to bring you to a happy place. You have the energy within.

So what if instead of making happiness the by-product of what we want, you make happiness your first goal? If you are writing your E-vites from a place of happiness, amazing things will RSVP. If you are starting from there, then the spot on the team, the perfect guy and a great group of friends are icing on the cake. We hope you like icing!

(instead of)
When I am popular ➜ then it will be easier to be happy

(switch it to . . .)
First I will be happy ➜ then it will be easier to be popular

So what is happiness and how do you get happy? Is happiness being on the cover of *Us Weekly*? The celebrity role models that society has put up for us to emulate seem to have everything you may think you want: fame, beauty, tons of cash, great clothes, a stylist, and their pick of hot guys. We don't want to mention any names, but many of them are lost. They don't seem that happy to us. If we could give you a foolproof recipe, we would. But being happy looks different for everyone. Some people think of it as exhilaration, others think of it as peace. Only you know what it looks like for you.

As an added bonus, being happy will help you attract what you want much more quickly. Read on. Once you've gotten yourself happier and radiating better energy, it's all about the fun of setting goals and watching them manifest. Have a little fun and be gentle with yourself as you start figuring out what you want. As soon as you get it, the rush you feel will be real but fleeting. It's just a matter of time before you'll be on to the next thing. The fun really is in the process of trying to achieve something.

Click Send on Authenticity

One of the qualities of truly happy people is authenticity. Watch a baby any day and you will see authenticity at its very best. Babies don't care what anyone thinks. They just are who they are. That used to be you when you were a baby—authentic pure energy. Get out a baby picture. Remember who you really are?

It is so easy to get caught up in all the rules and roles you have now. How you are supposed to dress, how you should act around your friends, what you are supposed to do to succeed in school, what to do to get into a good college. We are not suggesting you put on some Huggies, but we are saying to listen to your inner voice. Don't stifle yourself. Talk to your teachers, talk to your parents, say what you are really feeling, what you really mean. Not what you think people want to hear.

Perhaps the poster child for authenticity is Ellen Degeneres. After Ellen came out of the closet, her prime-time television sitcom was canceled, so she looked inward and stayed true to herself. She went back to her roots as a stand-up comedian. By staying authentic, Ellen sent out a clear E-vite: *I want to be successful on my own terms.* Her books, her talk show, her movie career, and her award-show gigs were the Universe's resounding RSVP: *Yes.* Watch her dance at the beginning of her show and you can see how comfortable she is in her own skin. She doesn't dance like you, she doesn't dance like us, she dances like Ellen.

To be truly happy, click send on your strengths. Remember what you were doing the last time you felt great? What comes naturally to you? Do you give great advice? Are you compassionate? Do you think outside the box? Take the time to get to know your inner strengths and then put yourself in situations that use those strengths whenever you can. For example, if you know that you'd love to take on a creative project, volunteer to help design the set at your next school play. If you work well as a team player, then sign up to play a team sport. If you are good at organizing and leading a group, run for student council. If you want help figuring out more things you are good at, check out Martin Seligman, PhD's, research at www.authentichappiness.org. His studies show that inner qualities like curiousity, originality, and kindness are things that can be enhanced every day and that through frequent use can help make you happier.

So when you put down the V-card, make a commitment to being happy, and honor who you really are, you will radiate love and confidence. Not only will these new ways of thinking lead to your own happiness, but they will also impact the people close to you. And who knows? Maybe your improved energy will radiate out to the world and make it a better place for all of us. Imagine how many problems, big and small, you will help solve just by shifting your energy.

→ *Go back to the playlist you just wrote. Write here the good feelings you think those things will bring you. When you're done, focus on those feelings for a minute.*

SEND		— ☐ X
TO:	The Universe	
FROM:	Feel Good Girl	
CC:	The Whole World	
RE:	How I feel about my playlist	

troubleshooting

The Dreaded "Peer Pressure"

Peer pressure: The phrase itself should be eliminated from use. It probably reminds you of a long assembly in a hot auditorium, where well-meaning student council members act out skits in which kids are offered drugs. But anyone who has ever left the house knows that peer pressure is a lot more complicated than that. As easy as it is sometimes to dismiss what your parents are asking you to do, it can seem impossible to dismiss your friends. The very idea of a group of friends implies that you all want the same things, right? Caution! When you are giving in to peer pressure, you are in effect clicking send on someone else's E-vite.

If we were to list here all the bad choices that we made as teenagers, the printing of this book would wipe out the rainforest. Having said that, we remember that some mistakes taught us a lot and proved to be very valuable. But doing something that is someone else's idea and does not feel right to you doesn't get you anywhere. In fact, it usually gets you further from knowing and then having what you really want.

Suppose you receive an e-mail with a strange-looking attachment from a friend's e-mail address. The subject line reads "Win A Cancun Vacation!" Let's get real . . . this e-mail has virus written all over it and your gut is telling you to delete it immediately! But visions of white sandy beaches and the MTV *Spring Break* beach house dance in your mind. Unlike the rest of the world, you usually spend your spring breaks working at the mall. This year could be different. Your curiosity gets the best of you and you open the e-mail anyway . . . just in case.

Like your PC, your self-confidence crashes when you ignore your inner guidance. E-vite: *I am untrustworthy.* RSVP: *Yes.* The most disappointing E-vites are the ones where you let yourself down! When a decision doesn't feel kosher to you, trust yourself and follow your gut.

We recommend you install your own "peer pressure" anti-virus software by thinking about uncomfortable situations in advance. Use the journal to script out how you want to react in tricky times. And think about where you stand on hot button issues like sex, drugs, and drinking, so you won't be forwarding other people's E-vites.

Gossip

Sure, we all love gossip. Sometimes it's hysterical to talk about who made a fool of themselves on the dance floor or who keeps making the same mistakes with guys. The important thing to remember when you think about gossip is that you are not just talking, you are creating. In

how the universe works: let's get started

all the time you spend repeating each other's stories, you are creating your own reality. Drama becomes the name of the game as the stories build, and pretty soon you are clicking send on some negative stuff you never intended.

Trust your gut about gossip. Notice that sick feeling you have after you've really just dished it over the drunken spectacle your friend put on at a party last week. For a while you felt really "on," and you had the great line "I hear she hooked up with the toilet bowl that night!" And you were the only one who knew the whole story about what happened when she finally got home. Your audience was captivated. But then comes that feeling, and what it is telling you is that you've clicked send on something you don't want. E-vite reads: *I'm not safe in this group.* RSVP: *Yes.*

The Focus Factor is working against you when you are gossiping. The most delicious thing about gossip is that it temporarily relieves your pain. If you were upset because your crush told your friend that he's not into you, then you are going to feel a little better telling and retelling the story about Amy, who got her period all over her white jeans in the cafeteria. At least that wasn't you! Well, brace yourself, because that heated and enthusiastic gossipfest you just had was focused on humiliation. It doesn't matter that it wasn't yours. RSVP: *Yes.*

Keep in mind that when you gossip, you are inviting more people into your life who gossip. Next time the gossip may be about you. If you want to surround yourself with more friends who don't gossip and backstab, then don't do these things yourself.

What if you spent all that time hashing and rehashing the details of something you all want. Maybe you'd be talking about that girl at school who seems to have it all going on. What it is about her that makes her so irresistible? Talk about it, analyze it, and invite it. Your gut will tell you how that feels.

If You Need It, You Won't Get It

One caveat to the Focus Factor: As you figure out what you want, remember that if you feel like you NEED what you want in order to be happy, the Universe will not be able to provide for you. E-vite reads: *Desperado.* Universe's reply: *Come to Your Senses.*

Remember last summer, when your mom's friend's kid suddenly developed a crush on you? First came the casual text messages. Random, but kind of cute. But then came the barrage of IMs and e-mails. The voice mails were soon to follow. This was no longer cute. The less interested you were, the more desperate he became. Before long, he couldn't make it through the day without stalking you in some way. All you wanted to do was hide.

Have you ever desperately wanted to be friends with someone? You were not going to be happy until the two of you were wearing matching BFF necklaces. Remember how you acted around her? Remember how you started laughing at her joke even before she got to the punch line? Our guess is that she didn't respond to your girl crush too enthusiastically.

The Universe smells desperation from a mile away, and it's a big turnoff. Plus the Universe can only return desperation with more desperation . . . and it becomes a downward spiral. If you are feeling desperate, chances are your thoughts are: *I must have this; if I don't I will be miserable!* (E-vite: *Miserable.* RSVP: *Yes*). See if you can bend your thoughts toward: *I can't wait to have this. I am going to feel so fulfilled/ relaxed/safe when I have it.* (E-vite: *Fulfilled/relaxed/safe.* RSVP: *Yes.*)

→ *Plan B. We've gone through what you want and why; now let's make sure we have a Plan B. Write a playlist of Plan B options that would feel nearly as good as your Plan A.*

SEND	— ☐ X
TO: The Universe	
FROM: Rolls with it	
CC: The Whole World	
RE: My Plan B	

putting the focus factor into practice

YOU'RE PROBABLY STARTING TO GET THE GIST of the Focus Factor: Your collective thoughts have energy that is like a stream of E-vites, constantly bringing the things you invite into your life. That's a pretty amazing concept, but like that violin on the floor of your closet, it's useless if you don't know how to use it. Let's talk about how you are going to make this work for you.

There is no way you could monitor every single thought you have. Anyway, you are too busy to sit around meditating over every thought, even if you wanted to. And frankly, that doesn't sound like very much fun anyway. Let's look at how to get in sync with what you want so that you can feel happy enough to let it all in.

Sync Up

Have you ever been to a club and the DJ decided to spin a new song? It sounds good. It makes you feel good. So you walk onto the dance floor. Maybe at it's a little awkward at first because it's new to you.

But eventually your body gets into the rhythm of the music and you start to dance. Maybe just a little toe tapping at first, but pretty soon it's effortless and you don't want to stop and you are even humming and singing along. When the rhythms change, you move with them, when the notes change, you harmonize. You are in sync with the music, moving with controlled abandon and it feels amazing.

You don't really have to go through all that rhythmic adjustment when it's a song you know really well. You hear the first two notes, jump up, and say, "This is my favorite song!" and you're dancing before you get onto the dance floor.

Okay. You're not at a club, but the message is the same. Getting in sync with the music is just like getting your energy in sync with your goal. Getting in sync with your goal is a critical step because it brings you what you want faster. Once you've aligned your energy with the energy of a goal, you get going with the flow, much in the same way you flow with a song that speeds up or slows down.

Different goals are just like different songs, and it takes a different amount of energy to get in sync with them. For example, if your friend asks you to ride your bike to the beach with her, you get on your bike and ride. You ride your bike to the beach all the time, you can picture the experience and know you can do it easily. You know that "song" and you're in sync. But if she asked you to play in a volleyball tournament with her when you got there, you'd need to do a little work. You don't play volleyball very often, you wonder who's going to be there and if you are going to have to be in your bathing suit. It's a new experience and, if you choose to dive in, you're going to need to get in sync.

Select a goal from your playlist as you would a song. You are the

DJ of your life and can decide which goal to spin and when. You can add your own beats or sample other songs to slightly change it. Or you can update your playlist when a goal no longer appeals to you. (Ever get tired of listening to the same song on your iPod?) You are in charge.

The dance floor is waiting. Make some room, Beyoncé and Shakira . . . Getting in sync with yourself and what you want is the best way to enjoy this dance floor we call life. So as Pink would say, *Get out on the dance floor now!*

What follow are shortcuts—think Cliffs Notes—to getting in the flow. The most successful people in our world use certain ways of thinking to get them in sync with their goals. Here are nine ideas to get you in sync with what you want.

1. Feel Good About Your Goal

The other day we were in a huge rush, trying to bake this cake that the Food Network made look so easy. We threw all the ingredients into the mixing bowl and suddenly realized that the recipe called for three eggs. All we had was an empty carton someone had left in the refrigerator.

The cake was inedible and we ended up tossing it in the garbage. Turns out the eggs had been a critical ingredient. Who knew?

We've talked a lot about making a commitment to feeling happy. But feeling good about what you want is like the eggs in the cake recipe. If you don't take the time to stir some "feeling good" into the creative process, you are going to end up with something you want to throw in the trash. Feeling good is all the evidence you need that your energy is positive and that your E-vites are flowing in a good way. Every time you have a warm and tingly feeling about something, rest assured that you just clicked send. If you feel good wanting something, it's coming. If you feel anxious or angry, then anxiety and anger are around the corner.

The most important thing you can do is to plan to feel good as much as possible, so that your E-vites don't get ruined. Have some extra feel-good strategies tucked away somewhere, in case you need them in a pinch.

→ *List five things that make you feel good no matter what. They can be anything: a song, a place you love, a particularly good kiss, the way your dog looks asleep on your bed, or the way your legs look in shorts. Anything.*

SEND	— ☐ X
TO:	The Universe
FROM:	Feeling Good
CC:	The Whole World
RE:	Five Feel-Good Standbys

One of the great pioneers of making the feel-good strategy work was Cinderella. Now, we have no proof that this is a true story, but it's been told so often that it might as well be. Cinderella was living the life of the eternally spilled coffee. Her parents were dead, her step monster was just that, and her stepsisters were a couple of first-class bitches. She was their slave, living in pure injustice with nearly no control of her circumstances. Almost anyone in this situation would be clicking send on: *Life sucks, I am trapped, there is no way out, and* (a personal favorite) *THIS IS SO UNFAIR!* RSVP: *Yes.*

But Cinderella took hold of what she could control: her thoughts and her energy. She sang while she scrubbed the floors, chatted with her bird friends while she poured the tea. She really made the best of the worst possible situation. She was clear and sure about what she wanted and was focused on where she wanted to be, not on where she was. You might remember the song she sings as she visualizes her dream. It wasn't *Someday My Life Won't Suck So Bad.* Or even *Someday Those Bitches Will Get Theirs.* It was an assured affirmation, sung with excitement: *Someday My Prince Will Come.* By the time she was done singing this song and imagining herself dancing at the palace, she could feel it. Her imagination had brought the energy of that experience into her life. She's even a bit surprised when she opens her eyes and finds that she's in her crappy little attic room dressed in last season's rags. She has sent the clearest possible E-vite. RSVP: *Yes.*

Take a minute to come up with one phrase that represents what you want to attract, a powerful phrase that you feel good about when you say it in your head. Example: *It's going to be great when I make the tennis team.* Let's call this your week's IM phrase, because here's the trick: Every time you get an IM, remember to think your thought. When you hear the IM beep on your computer, think the thought. We don't want to turn you into Pavlov's dog here, but getting in the habit of thinking that thought regularly will help you get in sync. Your IM phrase will be the first entry on your daily journal at the end of the book.

2. Write Your Story

· ·

Rescripting the story of your life as you are watching it unfold is the fastest possible way to focus your energy exactly on how you want things to be. In the journal there is a space for you to do this every day. Here's how Elisabeth made this work in high school.

elisabeth's story

While skimming through my old journals, I rediscovered a goal I had in ninth grade. I wanted to make new friends.

It was the fall of ninth grade and life was good. My BFF Mia and I were like Nicole and Paris in the first season of *The Simple Life.* We were on the same page about everything from boys to teachers to fashion strategies. I'm not sure what sparked it, but one day everything changed. We were eating lunch when Mia suddenly and inexplicably announced that she was now hanging out with the field hockey girls and slid her tray away from me, down to the opposite end of the cafeteria table to sit with them. In a matter of seconds, I had gone from cool to drool. My life was over as I knew it.

Who would I walk down the hall with? Who would sit next to me in English class? Where would I sit during lunch? These were the questions that consumed me for the next week. I was totally freaked out. Avoiding (i.e., hiding in the bathroom during lunch period and assembly) would only work for so long.

My parents, well meaning as they were, were of little help. "Girls are just mean and clique-y . . . ," my mom said. "In fact, I had a similar experience when I was your age." This was depressing news . . . clearly, being a loser ran in my family. I vowed that wouldn't be me.

So with plenty of time on my hands after school, and a room that needed to be purged of the vestiges of my depression (empty Dorito bags and Diet Coke cans), I stumbled across the diary my aunt had given me for my birthday. Little did I know the impact this would soon have. I had nothing better to do, so I began writing in my journal.

I thought about why I had been "dumped" and pledged that I would be a more considerate friend in the future. I composed a list of girls I was already a little friendly with and thought about what it might be like to hang out with them more. I wrote about what it would feel like to go to the parties I wanted to attend. Instead of sketching mean pictures of Mia and the field hockey girls (E-vite: *Mia is a bitch; I am isolated.* RSVP: *Yes*), I began sketching pictures of how I wanted my life to look. I wasn't sure how anything would play out, but I allowed myself to have fun thinking of the possibilities, and took things one day at a time. I wrote about the things in school that were going well, and how much I appreciated my dog. I reconnected with some of my summer camp friends. An article in *Seventeen* magazine suggested that I pretend that I was already "popular" and smile at people in the school hallways.

And soon, something strange began happening. The goals I was writing down started coming true. One day I was musing that it would be fun to be better friends with Jenny. Then the next thing you knew, I was invited to her birthday party. Thumb forward a few more entries, and I am writing about how much fun I had going to the movies with a group of new friends, (the ones on my initial list) and many were some of the most respected girls in the grade. A few entries later, I'm co-captain of the cheerleading squad and dating a really cute boy. By junior year, I had a lead in the school play and Mia and I were back on track. All of this stuff was really happening, just as I had scripted it. At the start of my senior year I was tapped into our school's super secret society, as one of only six girls chosen each year. Members take an oath of secrecy, but if you read carefully you just might find our secret buried in this book.

So did picking up a pencil change my life? I think it did. Why? In a sense, putting thoughts to paper is the equivalent of energy coming into matter. The physical act of writing stuff down forced me, the writer, to focus on the things I wanted with more intensity than just daydreaming. Using a journal enabled me to revisit what I wrote previously and visualize my desires again and again. The words themselves, letter by letter, vowel by vowel, supercharged my thoughts. Call it the Focus Factor on Red Bull.

You probably write down the things you want in other areas of your life without giving it much thought. Your last term paper probably began with an outline. Ever notice how quickly and efficiently you whiz through the grocery store when you have a list? It's not surprising that people who write down their goals are more likely to achieve them. Hell . . . look around you. Everything from your cell phone to your flatiron began as words on paper.

In case you haven't been paying attention, you are already writing your own life. So why not sit down and write it the way you want it to be? The journal portion of this book is your tool to plan a life that is fun and meaningful to you. Sit down every day to rescript your life. After you've written down what you want, write down exactly how it's going to be and how you are going to feel when you get it. Write until you feel yourself getting excited about it. This is such an incredibly powerful tool because your energy will immediately pick up the enthusiasm with which you write. You are clicking away. Send. Send. Send.

→ *Give it a try. Just start writing about how it's going to be when you get what you want. How will your life be different? How are you going to feel? Write the script for the next episode of VH1's* The Fabulous Life of . . . You.

SEND	— □ X

TO:	The Universe
FROM:	Scriptwriter
CC:	The Whole World
RE:	The Fabulous Life of . . . Me!

3. Visualize Your Course

Imagine this. You are Michelle Wie. You are about to compete on a golf course you've never played before, but you are not fazed at all. You already looked at pictures and contours of the course weeks before the tournament. Your sports psychologist and coach guided you through visualizations of all eighteen holes. You've practiced your stroke in your mind and watched video of it. You've quickly envisioned what it might be like to play on a wet course, just in case it rains the night before the tournament as the weatherman predicted. And of course you've visualized what it might be like when you tie for second on the tenth hole and take the lead on the sixteenth. The feel of the trophy cup in your hand is magnificent. You feel good! You feel confident! You are ready to kick some butt!

We hear it all the time on ESPN. Athletes often attribute their victories to their mental preparedness. We get the working out thing, but what does it mean to be "mentally fit" for competition? It is now common practice for athletes to engage in visualization strategies geared to enhance their performance.

Without positive visualization strategies, many athletes unconsciously use mental imagery and visualization to screw up their performance. They are more than likely replaying mistakes in their head, trying to fix what's wrong, not focusing on their skill set, and worried they will embarrass themselves. Not only does this way of thinking exhaust them during competition, but it can lead to an appearance on *Best of Sports Bloopers.* Focusing on messing up ensures more messing up will follow. Positive visualization changes all this. It fills athletes with energy and confidence and enables them to win!

What's that? You're not a professional athlete? Sorry. Let's say you want a group of friends that you can count on. Close your eyes and picture yourself among them. Where are you? What would it feel like to know you always had weekend plans to just fall into? What if you could walk away from the lunch table and know that no one was talking about you? How would it feel to know they always had your back? Imagine it and draw a picture of this scene or make a collage out of magazine pictures of groups of friends. Doing this, you are feeling great and feeling so close to being a part of it all. All of this focus is sending out a powerful stream of E-vites. They read *Great friends!* RSVP: *Yes!*

Here is another example. You made some careless mistakes on last week's algebra quiz. You have another one lurking around the corner and have found yourself saying while studying, "UGH! I can't screw up those equations again. If I don't get an A, my average will be ruined!" E-vite reads *Screw up!* Instead, try saying, "Won't it be awesome to feel cool, calm, and collected the day of the test?" Or imagine yourself turning in your test feeling like you completed it easily and efficiently. RSVP says: *Ace.*

In addition to visualizing in your mind, take a minute to tape or draw a picture of what you want in your journal. Our friend Valerie, who isn't exactly Rembrandt, drew stick figures under a shining sun to thwart the huge rainstorm that was forecast for her sweet sixteen. It worked.

So here's the big exercise: Design your Facebook page. No, we know you've already done that. But that's all about how your life *is*. Now design one here to reflect how you want your life to be. Have a little fun with it. How do you look? Who's been writing all over your Facebook wall? What does it say? Write about some of the things on your playlist as if they already happened. Let's say you want better friends. Rewrite your friend list. Who just asked you to be friends with them? What network do you want to be on? You are visualizing and adding data to your future. If you want to improve your swimming stats—paste on an article about the girl who won at the state swimming meet, but type your name over hers. Do this collage style or get out your markers—be creative and look at it often.

→ *Design your dream Facebook page. Get into the details—be specific!*

MY DREAM FACEBOOK PAGE

4. Get Grounded

We aren't talking about the time your parents ran into your friend Estrella at the supermarket when you were supposed to be "going to the movies with Estrella." We're talking about you grounding your energy. Just like the electrical appliances in your home need to be grounded to be safe and effective, so must your energy be grounded for you to use the Focus Factor. Once your energy is grounded, you can clearly focus on getting what you want and not simply react as life unfolds before you. What's the difference between feeling grounded and not? Check out how different these two mornings feel.

A grounded morning: *You set your alarm early and take time to breathe deeply, thinking about the day ahead. You take your day planner and look at your "to do" list, which you organized last night. These little goals feel achievable to you and you imagine how great you will feel when you have completed them. You look at your "Big Goal" and you visualize and get in sync with it. You look at your "feel good" thoughts page and your "Facebook" page and seeing these things gives you a little boost. You are beginning the day in a clear-headed way and you feel relaxed. You know what you want.* E-vite: I feel good. RSVP: Yes. Good things are on their way.

A frazzled morning: *Where the hell is your favorite T-shirt? You start the day searching through your clothes in a pile on the floor. You can't find anything unwrinkled and end up wearing a shirt that's a little too tight and jeans that are a little last year. You run out the door and then realize you forgot your planner and have to go back inside and get it.*

You haven't looked at it in a few days and have a sinking feeling you
forgot to do something. Is your economics project due today? Or is it
due tomorrow? Are you supposed to give Marina a ride home from
school? E-vite: I feel out of control. *RSVP:* Yes. *Look out!*

Of course, it is up to you how you want to manage your time,
and maybe there is a part of you that enjoys the excitement of
procrastinating and trying to juggle things in your head. Just keep
in mind that it is much easier to start off the day with balanced
energy. That way, good things are coming your way all day. And if a
problem happens to creep up, you can quickly deal with it and get
back in balance.

Let's just say Susie Bitch makes a rude comment to you. If you
are having a grounded day, you will be able to easily recover and get
your energy in balance. Maybe you will think, *Wow . . . that sucked, but*
you know something . . . It makes me realize that I want to have friends
who appreciate me. In fact, Tess and Paloma do like me the way I am and
I am psyched to hang out with them at field hockey practice today. When
you are feeling grounded, it's much easier to bring your focus back to
what you want and not get distracted.

If you are already feeling frazzled and distracted, you might not
have the presence of mind to rewrite your E-vites before you click
send. You might start crying or say something bitchy that you'll regret
later because you do not have the sense of calm necessary to keep it
in perspective.

One of the best ways to get grounded is to get organized. Let's
face it, there are always going to be things that you have to do that

aren't your favorites. But if you make sure you carve out time to do the things that are important to you, the other stuff won't seem so painful. Create "to do" lists and track assignments for school. We suggest you use a day planner to keep a "to do" list. Don't have one? Of course you do. Turn to the back of this book and look in your journal. (Oh, you're welcome!) This way you can really focus on what you want and make sure you have time to make it happen.

One last thing on grounding: The only thing that keeps your spirit on the ground is—yes, you guessed it—your body. Be kind. Treat it well, get enough sleep, feed it things that help it thrive, take it for a walk. Being grounded is really the most practical piece of this puzzle. And if you are starving or exhausted or hung over, it's really hard to feel like you are starting the day from a place of balance. Treat yourself well so that all of your pieces and parts will cooperate to get you what you want.

5. Get Some 'Tude

We're not talking "attitude" here. This is not permission to tell your teacher where she can shove that pop quiz. The type of 'tude we're talking about is "gratitude." Plain and simple, having a sense of gratitude is a shortcut to feeling good. Studies have shown that writing down positive aspects of our lives and appreciating the things we take for granted can improve your mood.

Don't worry. We're not asking you to kid yourself into jumping for joy over your broken leg. Instead, use the journal to jot down a gratitude list each day of the things you feel happy to have. It's so simple, and one of your most powerful weapons in your feeling-good arsenal.

Feeling grateful immediately focuses your attention on something that you want. If you are feeling frustrated because you sprained your ankle at the track meet, you might turn it around by taking a second to focus on these things:

1. *I am grateful that it's just a sprain.*

2. *I am grateful that I am strong and fast enough to have made the track team at all.*

3. *I am grateful that I live in a place where kids have extra time for sports.*

Suddenly your energy about your ankle is better. You've put it in perspective and your energy is moving you toward healing.

If you are having a tough time getting started, just look around you. Ask yourself where you would be without your cell phone. E-mail enables you to forgo a trip to the post office. You don't have to handwrite your term paper. Your house has indoor plumbing and your waterproof mascara doesn't run. We have it so much better than most of the world. Done with today's list already! Feeling grateful is just a shortcut to having good energy. A few seconds of focus on what makes your life good invites more good stuff into it.

Look at the people around you. Even the most irritating ones have good qualities you can appreciate. Your mom is actually a pretty good listener, despite her annoying questions. Your dad may tell the corniest jokes, but he lets you borrow his car. Your brother has an amazing ear for music. Your teacher knows you exist and recommended you for the school paper. The gossip in your study hall (when she's not talking about you) really does keep things lively.

Our friend Christine just broke up with The Biggest Jerk Ever (not his real name). She could dwell on all the horrible things he's done, and the fact that she now doesn't have a prom date. E-vite: *Horrible jerk, lame prom.* RSVP: *Yes.* She would be attracting another jerk and an uninspired social life. But she has decided to put an end to that by offering gratitude. She is grateful for the fact that he taught her how to snowboard. She is grateful that breaking up has enabled her to spend more time reconnecting with her amazing group of friends. She feels empowered by her new independence and enthusiastically awaits the better guy that she knows she is going to meet. E-vite: *I am strong and it's going to be great.* RSVP: *Yes.*

The greatest rewards come when you can smile in the face of your challenges. There are no accidents, and everything happens for a reason. So next time you are benched for the biggest game of the season, see it as a wake-up call and ask yourself, "What am I supposed to be learning from this?" When you can find something to appreciate even on a bad day, you've got it made. Your challenging days will be a lot easier, your good days will be more joyful, and you'll be attracting more of what you want!

Be sure to list them every day, because the act of focusing on them will shift your energy to a place where you are attracting more things you want. Try it here.

→ *List four things you are grateful for.*

SEND		— □ X
TO:	The Universe	
FROM:	So Grateful	
CC:	The Whole World	
RE:	Thanks!	

6. Act Like It's a Done Deal

Have you ever gotten great news before everybody else? You feel great, you have put out your best energy, you're just waiting for everyone else to find out. Whatever it is that you want, act like it's already happened. Walk down the red carpet like Melissa Rivers just whispered to you that she's already seen the inside of the envelope. You won! Walk around in total certainty that what you want to happen is about to happen any minute. Feel the excitement knowing that your phone is going to ring with the best possible news. At that moment, you are sending out the clearest possible E-vite because you are already appreciating what it's like to have your desire. You are already living in the feeling of it. You are totally in sync. Doubt, fear, and anxiety cloud an E-vite. When you are certain that your wish has been granted, those things fade away and, guess what? You've got mail! RSVP: *Yes.*

Our hearts go out to Jen, but how could Brad and Angelina *not* have hooked up? While they were filming the movie *Mr. and Mrs. Smith,* their sole job was to act like they were this superhot married couple. They spent hours on the set trying to act as if they were wildly attracted to each other. Then, as if that wasn't enough to summon the energy, they did the *Vanity Fair* photo shoot of the two of them in domestic bliss with a bunch of kids. Is it any wonder that just a few short years later they are in fact a superhot married couple with a bunch of kids?

Take a minute to act like it's a done deal. If it's your dream to be a doctor, write your name down with the letters "MD" after it. Or write a thank-you note to Paula Abdul for her support of your performance on *American Idol.* You really wouldn't have won that recording contract without her. Look your crush in the eye and say to yourself, "Yeah, you know you want me." It will change your energy and get you in sync quickly.

7. Photoshop It

Touch up your past experiences as you would with Photoshop. Maybe a little red-eye reduction here to make it less emotional. Or maybe you crop out the girl who spilled grape punch all over your white prom dress right as you were walking in. Don't dwell on what's already happened if it's something you don't like. Leave its energy behind, so you can stop attracting more of it. Dump out your baggage; just bring the good stuff with you.

If you are still breaking into a cold sweat every time you remember the night you went through an entire party with a big chunk of lettuce wedged between your two front teeth, you are still clicking send on mortification. Thoughts and memories can kind of sneak up on you. There you are, minding your own business, eating a cobb salad, when the whole scene comes back to you. The hundreds of times you laughed with your mouth open, and the "seductive" smile you flashed at your crush as you were saying good-bye. It wasn't until you got home and went to brush your teeth that you saw it. Your heart starts to race when you replay this, and you are mortified all over again.

Photoshop that experience and give it a makeover. Rewrite the story that appears in your mind, take yourself out, change the circumstances. Or just airbrush out that big head of lettuce. Turn it into anything that you feel like you can look at with a less charged reaction every time it pops up. If you can do that, you'll notice that it will start popping up much less frequently.

8. Write Some Thoughts to Click Send On

Consciously compose your E-vites. When know you are in a situation where normally your E-vites would look like #$%!, you want to turn it around before all that smelly stuff flies back your way. Grab a thought that is better. Make a list of all the good thoughts you can muster about the thing you really want. List things that you really believe; don't b.s. yourself. For example, if you write: "*I play tennis like Venus Williams*," you are not going to believe it because you double fault more times than not. Chances are that reading it will make you think, *No, I'm not, I suck,* and oops! You just clicked send.

Try to come up with positive things (thoughts to click send on) that you can really believe and list them in your journal. Test yourself after you write it. Did I believe this? Do I feel good when I read it? These might work:

1. *I am better than I was last year.*

2. *I practiced all summer.*

3. *There are three more spots to be filled on the team this year.*

4. *I love the way I feel in my tennis skirt.*

Remember Masaru Emoto's study about attaching the words to the water bottles? The study showed that the written word has energy and can be very powerful. By writing down these more positive thoughts, even if they are only slightly more positive, you create words with energy and your energy will become more positive just for having written them.

→ *Write five thoughts about your goal that would be great to click send on.*

SEND		_ □ X
TO:	The Universe	
FROM:	Big Clicker	
CC:	The Whole World	
RE:	Thoughts to Click Send On	

9. Get Some Action!

Now that you've set the stage with all your "feeling good" strategies, make sure your actions match your goals. Let's revisit our old friend Cinderella. Imagine this had happened:

As the coach pulls away from the house, Cinderella kicks off her glass slippers and notices a blister forming on her heel already. Never one for high heels (let alone slippery, unforgiving glass stilettos), she nervously ponders how she can take a step, let alone do a box step. Hmmm. There is a flask of something in the pocket of the door, and Cinderella thinks, Why not? . . . Maybe just one sip will calm my nerves. Isn't that what people do pre-Ball anyway? Cinderella has never had a drop of alcohol before, but feeling a little anxious and in a festive mood, she decides . . . Why not? (Note to parents: There is no drinking age in Happily Ever After-land).

Alas, by the time she arrives at the palace, Cinderella is stretched out in the back of the coach, feeling dizzy and nauseous. Instead of meeting the prince, she barely makes it to the palace toilette, before throwing up all over her gown. Barely remembering the royal flush, she passes out, misses her ride home at midnight, and ends up doing the walk of shame in her bare feet and tattered dress.

Thank goodness this didn't happen. Cinderella knew enough to keep her eyes on the prize and seized every opportunity to move her dream forward. When the prince asked her to dance, she said yes.

She smiled big and worked those high heels. She chatted with the prince and curtseyed her way into his heart.

The moral of this story is that you can spend lots of time visualizing your success and setting yourself up to succeed, but if you don't follow up your E-vites with the right actions, all your work will go right down the royal toilette.

The Universe is absolutely willing to do its part. And if you are willing to feel good and get in sync with your goals, it will most likely deliver. But—here's the part that may burst your bubble—you have to help it along. If your dream is to play in a band and you've never had a guitar lesson, then the Universe can't help. If you want to have more friends but you keep your head down and don't talk to anybody, then the Universe can't help. If it's your dream to dance for the New York City Ballet and you've never put on a tutu, then the Universe can't help. You have to get in the way of your dream before it zooms by. In short, if you want to be a dancer, dance. And feel great doing it.

One thing that we've often noticed in our own lives is that as soon as you really get in sync with your goal and start feeling excited about it, you find yourself taking action without much effort at all. When you are really in sync with wanting to feel healthy, you feel like going for a run. When you set the goal to make the dean's list and start to imagine what it would feel like to achieve it, you might find yourself studying in a clearer, more focused way.

I am sure you've heard people say, "They have the most amazing house! They're so lucky!" or "You're going to Penn State on a full ride? You're so lucky." When we hear comments like that, we always remember that expression "The harder I work, the luckier I get." Your amazing life won't be a result of luck or a lightning bolt. It will be a result of finding happiness within your self and meeting the Universe halfway with your actions.

→ *Make a To-Do List. What can you commit to doing that will line you up with your goal? How can you meet the Universe halfway?*

SEND		_ ☐ X
TO:	The Universe	
FROM:	Halfway There	
CC:	The Whole World	
RE:	My To-Dos	

special topics: let's focus

YOU GET THE CONCEPT, you have the tools to get in sync, now let's apply them to what's really going on in your life. Take the quiz at the beginning of each section to determine what kinds of E-vites you are already sending out. Then read on to hear what girls have been telling us about how they want to change their lives. Can you relate? Then take our advice to heart.

At the end of each section is an E-vite Rewrite. We have taken some common negative E-vites and have reframed them to invite something more positive. Use them as a reference tool, an encyclopedia of better energy, if you will. Read through them and see which ones apply to you. Feel free to add your own.

your love(less) life

Pop Quiz: Test Your Romance Energy

1. You heard that your crush will be asking you to the Homecoming Dance. Two days later, when he hasn't called, you . . .

   A. *panic! Then discuss with your friends why he hasn't followed through.*

   B. *dress to impress. If he still doesn't call, text him 24/7.*

   C. *take your focus off your cell phone by practicing your lines for the school play.*

2. The boy you are into is into someone else. You think:

   A. *His loss. But maybe if I continue to text him, he will eventually see the light.*

   B. *It's no wonder. She's hot and I'm not.*

   C. *His loss, but I know I am a really cool girl. It'll be awesome to find a guy who sees that.*

3. The guy you like has become an octopus and a sloppy kisser. He's always all over you and you are finding it kind of gross. You . . .

A. *pretend you are really into it. You are lucky he even likes you.*

B. *tell him what you do like by making it into a bit of a fun game.*

C. *start to tell him what you like, but chicken out and say "just kidding."*

4. Your best friend tells your crush how much you are into him. You . . .

A. *are devastated that your BFF did this to you. And how could you have been so stupid as to have trusted her?*

B. *will keep your friend's wagging tongue in mind next time you have a secret. The fact your crush knows of your interest may help you get him to notice you.*

C. *pretend it doesn't bother you now, but remind her about it next time she spills the beans.*

5. The guy that seemed to like you last week won't give you the time of day. You think:

A. *That's okay. There are plenty of other people I like hanging out with.*

B. *OMG! I've gotten totally FAT!*

C. *I bet something's going on in his life. I hope I didn't do anything to annoy him.*

6. The boy you like treats you differently when he's with his friends. But when you are alone, it's all about you. You think:

A. *I can totally deal with this. Then whine about it to your friends nonstop.*

B. *Yes, it's annoying. But I really don't need him to give me his full attention 24/7.*

C. *Next time he blows me off, I'm going to kick his butt.*

7. The boy you are into is a huge sports fanatic. You'd rather watch anything but. The next time he flips on the game, you . . .

A. *make a deal. It's hockey today,* Grey's Anatomy *tomorrow. Then throw on your jersey and break out the chips and salsa. This could be sort of fun.*

B. *groan loudly and stomp out of the room, while mumbling under your breath, "I hate hockey."*

C. *say, "Oh, goody," and fake smile your way through the first half until you pass out from sheer exhaustion.*

8. You are going out to dinner with the parents of the boy you like for the first time. You think:

A. *They are going to think I'm a pretty great person.*

B. *They seem so cool. I wish I had something to wear other than this stupid dress.*

C. *I just know I'll get food stuck in my teeth and no one will tell me.*

9. The boy you are seeing is "really good friends" with his ex-girlfriend. The next time they go to the mall together, you . . .

A. *have your friend go undercover and shadow them. Her cell takes great pictures, so she may be able to collect evidence they are more than friends.*

B. *act as if their quality time together doesn't bother you, and then throw it in his face the next time you argue.*

C. *tell him how you really feel and see what he does.*

10. You can cut a rug, but the boy you like dances like he's having convulsions. At the next party, when your favorite 50 Cent song comes on, you . . .

A. *run! If he can't find you, he can't embarrass you on the dance floor.*

B. *dance with your friends and box him out of your circle.*

C. *admit to yourself that you're a bit embarrassed. Then hit the dance floor and enjoy the great music. Maybe he'd be open to a dance lesson or two from you!*

Score it: Give yourself the appropriate number of points for each answer.

1. a = 3, b = 2, c = 1	**6.** a = 2, b = 1, c = 3
2. a = 2, b = 3, c = 1	**7.** a = 1, b = 3, c = 2
3. a = 3, b = 1, c = 2	**8.** a = 1, b = 2, c = 3
4. a = 3, b = 1, c = 2	**9.** a = 3, b = 2, c = 1
5. a = 1, b = 3, c = 2	**10.** a = 3, b = 2, c = 1

special topics: let's focus

10-14: *Congratulations! You're cool as a cucumber. You know who you are, and that makes you a guy magnet. You are optimistic and playful, you know it's going to happen, and you don't stress too much about when.*

15-25: *You are getting there. Guys see you as fun and confident, but it's usually because a lot of the time you are putting on an act to seem fun and confident. This won't hold up over time. Focus a little more on what you want, rather than bending to be what you think he wants. You're so close!*

26-30: *Pay careful attention to the rest of this section, because we want to help you rewrite some of the E-vites you are sending out, namely:* I am nothing without you *and* If you don't like me I will cease to exist.

This Is the Deal

. . . .

Life really isn't the way it is in the movies. Except that there's a lot of drama surrounding romance, countless broken hearts, and millions of miscommunications. Okay, scratch that. Life really is a lot like the movies. Except that you feel it so much more deeply.

When navigating the boy-girl jungle, it's best to bring a compass along with your lip gloss. Like a compass that's always pointing you North, use your gut as a compass to help you gauge your energy. You'll wonder how to get the guy you like to like you, and then once you've got him you'll wonder how to keep him. Cameron and Justin never figured it out, neither did Kirsten and Jake. Adam and Rachel couldn't make it last, and Jen and Vince . . . you know the story. (Let's face it. They hooked up on the set of a movie called *The Break Up*. What did you expect?) Let your gut be your guide and trust it to help you figure out what you want, why you want it, and if you really even want it with *him*.

One not-to-be-named-co-author-of-a-book-you-may-be-reading-right-now totally blew it in high school. Against all laws of nature, Super Cute Cool Guy somehow ended up being her boyfriend. All his friends were friends with all her friends, they all went to the same parties and hung out at the same beaches. It was like *The O.C.* before Marissa was killed. But she was so freaked out to have this cute boyfriend that she tried to cuff him and keep him all to herself. At parties, she'd cling to him and get mad if he averted his attention for an instant. His friends made fun of him for being whipped. In short, she was rushing this guy into middle age at sixteen and potentially ruining all his fun. He knew enough to get out to save himself, and she spent the rest of junior year mourning the one that got away. Literally, got away.

So what happened? If she'd asked herself what she wanted, she'd have said that she wanted to be with him and to feel comfortable and confident in her own skin. E-vite: *Cool guy's cool girlfriend.* RSVP: *Yes.* Instead, she was focused on how entirely insecure she felt at that present moment. She was in a full panic about herself and her ability to hold on to this cool guy so she smothered him. E-vite: *He's going to leave.* RSVP: *Yes.*

With romance in particular there are so many conflicting thoughts and feelings (not to mention the fact that the feelings are supercharged!) that it's easy to attract what you don't want. Read on to hear what some other girls are clicking send on—call them E-mails from the Edge. We'll try to use some of our tricks to help turn around their E-vites.

· ·

Last week I really thought I had my golden opportunity. Because of overcrowding in our cafeteria I actually ended up having lunch at the same table as the hottest guy on the lacrosse team. I have always had the biggest crush on him (who doesn't?) but I feel like I really pulled it off. I was totally normal the whole time and we had really good conversation. I felt like we connected and that maybe he liked me. After stressing over this all week with my friends, I decided to wait with a bunch of people, in a casual way, after Friday night's lacrosse game when the team came off the field. My friends were really excited for me and we all held our breath as he walked our way. He said hi to a couple of my friends and stopped to talk to one. He acted like I wasn't even there! My best friend said, "Cal, you know Heather, right?" and motioned to me. He turned to me and said, "No, nice to meet you." I felt like I would die. What's wrong with me?

↩ **Reply:**

· ·

Yikes! This is one of those situations that can wrestle your self-esteem to the ground. You wonder what is so unmemorable about you. How is it possible to be so obsessed with someone and have them so, well, unobsessed with you? Assuming you are not really just someone's imaginary friend, let's break this down before you start clicking send on: *I am not here.*

The first thing you need to do is figure out what you want and WHY. Chances are, if you've only had one conversation with this guy, you can't be totally sure he's exactly what you're looking for.

Maybe you like him for the way he looks, and the stuff you see him do. In a sense, you like what he represents to you. He's athletic, he's confident, he's popular. And you like him because you want to bring these things into your life. How do those qualities make you feel? Most of us want joy, security, satisfaction, love. So let's loosen up the noose you've thrown around this guy's neck and focus on what you really want. Do you want to feel love, do you want to fit in and feel secure? Do you want to feel comfortable in your own skin? Do you want to be with someone who will help bring this out in you? Focus on those things and how great it will feel to have them. How great will that feel? E-vite: *Love, acceptance, security.* RSVP: *Yes.*

TO: **Click!**
FROM: **Suffering From Chronic Jerk Syndrome**
RE: **Help!**

. . . .

My first real boyfriend, Milo, turned out to be a total jerk—he cheated on me, he lied to me, you name it. I didn't get over him until I finally hooked up with Blake. He was really cool and seemed totally into me until I found him in the bathroom getting cozy with my cousin on Valentine's Day. I was totally devastated and swore off guys altogether. Who wouldn't, right? When I finally met Carl, I was psyched. He was so cool and really seemed to like me. I dove in again, only to find out (AFTER I'd already hooked up with him!) that he totally had a girlfriend already. Are all guys like this? Can none of them be trusted? It seems like they are all just out for themselves and looking for a better deal. Should I give up on guys altogether?

↩ **Reply:**

. . . .

This is really the perfect example of why people make the same mistakes over and over again. You don't have chronic bad taste in guys. It's just that you keep clicking send on the same old crap. And why wouldn't you? Let's review: You met the first jerk, then fretted over what a lying, cheating jerk he was. (Which, we agree, he was.) By the time you finished that first brooding pint of Chunky Monkey, you'd honed all of your focus on lying, cheating jerk. Over days and months and endless conversations with all your friends you rehashed what a lying, cheating jerk he is. RSVP: *Yes*, again and again.

We think that Carrie Underwood almost had it right when she took the key to the side of her boyfriend's 4-wheel drive. She got mad, got it out of her system, and then resolved that the next time he cheated, it would not be on her. She stated very clearly by the end of the song that she wanted to click send on an entirely different kind of guy. We say she "almost" got it right, because, well, trashing someone's car is property damage and she could go to jail. We've heard that's not a great place to meet nice guys.

If you have really decided that Spencer from *The Hills* and Jason from *Laguna Beach* aren't for you, try this next time: Get mad, finish the pint, and then be done. See if you can take your seriously bruised ego and treat it to a little energy makeover. Write a personal ad to yourself. Write your story of your future love life. Describe the kind of guy you want. Won't it be nice when you meet a guy who is hot and fun to be around but that feels comfortable enough in his own skin not to have to flex his man muscle for every girl at school? Work on this for a while until you get kind of excited about meeting him. If you get a clear idea about what you want and deserve in your head, you won't fall for the next shady character that comes your way. Click send on: *I deserve to be treated well.*

TO: **Click!**
FROM: **Buddy**
RE: **Help!**
. . . .

My best guy friend thinks I am totally cool. He writes all over my Facebook wall, he laughs at all my jokes, he texts me all the time at school, he even noticed when I got a new haircut. The problem is that I'm a lot of fun to hang out with, but I'm not really the kind of girl that guys want to go out with. He goes out with tons of other girls and doesn't seem interested in anything more than being friends with me. How can I make him see me that way?

↩ **Reply:**
. . . .

Ahh, the old "he doesn't like you That Way." (A more annoying phrase? We cannot think of one.) So all that attention was just a big tease because he'd rather punch you in the arm than smooch you on the lips. What's wrong with you? Did you go too far buying all those boy jeans last fall?

No. Before you click send on *I am unattractive and definitely not romance material. I should start picking out names for the ninety-eight cats I am going to grow old with,* let's think about what you do have. You have a friendship, which is where most romance starts out and ends up anyway. You have a great personality and a rockin' new look. Maybe this guy hasn't clued into your vibe yet, but that's just one guy. Maybe he's known you so long that it just hasn't occurred to him yet to look at you that way. But, what? Are you uglier than Ugly Betty? Far from it! Get out there and have a great time. Find another crush and remember that life is long. When he sees you out there dating, feeling great about yourself, and having fun, he may have one of those Hollywood moments where you'll go into slow motion and he'll see the way the sun reflects off of your hair and he'll realize that you've been there all along! It's not impossible.

In the meantime, focus on what feels good. You are obviously the kind of girl that he likes to hang out with because he hangs out with you all the time. You have a good friend and there are a hundred other guys to go out with. You are just going to enjoy your life and yourself and who knows, maybe he'll have a change of heart. Or maybe you'll meet someone cooler in the meantime. *Feel good about what you want,* not desperate. Broaden your search a little. It doesn't have to be this guy. Have fun imagining what it would be like to be with a guy who's really into you. E-vite: *I'm cool, I'm happy, I'm super datable.* If you feel good, good things will happen. RSVP: *Yes.*

Let's try to rewrite your E-vite. (You should do this with every problem, but we're going to do it for you here). This guy is one of a million guys like him, so let's not make too much of him. The worry for us is that you have decided that you are "not the kind of girl that guys want to go out with." Who told you that? Do all guys want the same kind of girl? That's impossible. Can you come up with a new way to think about yourself that you can believe?

- *I am really fun to be with.*

- *Lots of guys like spending lots of time with me.*

- *I like the way I am.*

- *Someone else will too.*

If any of those work for you, click send. Remember that you can save new beliefs over old ones. It's never too late to start fresh.

TO: **Click!**
FROM: **Totally Jealous**
RE: **Help!**
. . . .

It's finally happened! My longtime crush finally likes me and we are totally dating. He hangs out at my house after school all the time. All of our friends come over and we go swimming. My BFF Jamie isn't hooking up with anyone, but she always comes along and hangs out with all of us. It's perfect, right? Well, lately I've noticed that my boyfriend has been paying a crazy amount of attention to Jamie. She's superhot and never puts anything on over her bikini after she gets out of the pool. I'm not exactly equipped to compete with her in a bikini, if you know what I mean. I want her to stop coming over altogether. I feel panicked—it's like two nightmares in one! How can I make this stop?

↩ **Reply:**
. . . .

Most girls would stop inviting the hot friend and her long legs around and, in the meantime, spend every moment with their boyfriend bad-

special topics: let's focus

mouthing everything about her from her clothes to her tennis swing. You have to protect yourself, right?

Wrong. We say that Jamie's sudden absence, if your crush is in fact interested, would make her the most mysterious thing since Ashlee Simpson's new nose. More than anything, guys love a chase. Don't make him wonder where she is and how he can hunt her down. Bad-mouthing anything about her draws more attention to her and points out to him the fact that you aren't as cool as he thought you were. E-vite: *BFF is hot; I am insecure.* RSVP: *Yes.*

It's also time for you to *get some 'tude.* You are completely missing what you already have because you are so worried about what might happen. The truth is that he likes *you.* He's your boyfriend, not hers. Focus on the reasons you think he likes you. Focus on the things you like about yourself. But, by all means, do not focus on the myriad ways you don't think you measure up to Jamie. If you do, you won't measure up at all.

Bad news really has no place in this book, but let's get a reality check. There's always going to be competition. If you are so beautiful that birds sing a sweet tune when you walk down the street, chances are there is some chick in Sweden who makes the birds actually break into "Your Body is a Wonderland." Should you one day work out at the gym hard enough that your legs are featured on the cover of *Hot Legs Magazine,* chances are that there are another pair out there to give you a literal run for your money. And if, someday, you become rich enough to show up at the polo matches in a limo, you will meet someone there who flew in by helicopter. The point? There is no end game here. You are not going to win at love by competing. You are going to win by enjoying the game, figuring out who you are, and being authentic.

Take Sarah Jessica Parker. SJP is not the stereotypical Miss America. She is not a perfect 5'9". She was not raised rich. Her success stems from her talent, her focus, and her authenticity. We haven't actually met her, but the E-vite we get from her every time we pick up a magazine is: *I am me! I am exactly the me that I want to be! I feel beautiful!* RSVP: *Yes.*

TO: **Click!**
FROM: **Lip-locked**
RE: **Help!**

. . . .

My crush and I are going to be at the same party Friday night. What if one thing leads to another and we kiss? I am worried that I will be the worst kisser ever. I'm not just being dramatic—this summer at camp I actually was! I really liked this guy named Alex and we snuck out one night to meet by the lake. It was really romantic and we talked for a long time. Finally, he kissed me. It was kind of weird at first and then I felt like I was getting the hang of it. I went back to my cabin so excited and happy. The next day he told everyone at camp that I was the worst kisser ever. I have no clue what I'm doing and I don't want to gross another guy out.

↩ **Reply:**

. . . .

So you're pretty sure you came off like a St. Bernard puppy the first time. Time for panic to set in. You've probably practiced on your little sister's Elmo doll, but it's creepy how he keeps saying "tickle me." It feels like everyone is confident in this area but you. What are you supposed to do with your arms and how do you manage them and

special topics: let's focus

your mouth and your potentially stinky onion dip breath? OMG!! There is no WAY you're going out on Friday.

Take a deep breath. Everybody's been there. But let's take a quick look at the current E-vite: *I am gross. He is going to think I am a disaster!* No need to wait for the RSVP, it's yes. You are doing a great job setting up this experience to be exactly how you think it is going to be. Chances are that with all this panicked build up, you'll be even more nervous as those lips start to close in on you.

Has anyone you know ever attended a fully accredited kissing academy? No? Then how is it that people have been smoldering in such passionate kisses (and, gasp! more) since before they actually discovered fire? So let's not take something perfect and natural and ruin it like Paris did to her Chihuahua. And remember, unlike your exploits with Elmo, you're not going to be alone. This is not a monologue. The whole point of kissing a guy is that you like him and want to be with him. So be *with* him and you two can figure it out. An aside—sadly, he's not reading this book. He's probably bought four different kinds of revolting body sprays in the past few days and is clicking send on his own garbage too. Let's give him a break, too, and not take this too seriously.

Try *visualizing your course.* Imagine the kiss, think of other kisses you've seen in movies. Don't focus on the mechanics of it, just on the feeling of it. Try to click send on this: *I really like this guy. I am going to be happy and relaxed and try to have a sense of humor about this. I'll know what to do.*

You can also incorporate a little *get some action* into getting this action. First of all, skip the onion dip and brush your teeth before you go out. Pay attention to him and what he's doing when you kiss. Don't dive in and splash around like you're drowning. You'll probably get the hot lips award by next summer.

e-vite rewrite

Let's try to rewrite some of these thoughts, so they are sending out the E-vite that you want.

CURRENT E-VITE	E-VITE REWRITE
No guys like me.	*I'd like a great guy to like me. Maybe I'll meet one at camp.*
All the guys who like me are geeks.	*It's cool that some guys like me. Can't wait to meet one that I like.*
All the guys are so into the new girl. She is totally fake. Why can't they see that?	*Not every guy is into her. There are lots of people who like me, too.*
It seems like everybody in this world is paired up but me.	*It's so good to see so many people happy together. When the time is right, I'll have that too.*
Why do all the popular guys like the same bitchy girls?	*It'll feel amazing to be with someone who appreciates my authenticity.*
I'm not the type of girl that guys usually like.	*I want a guy to like me for who I am. I have beautiful and unique qualities about me, too.*

special topics: let's focus

your so-called social life

Pop Quiz: Test Your Friend Energy

1. Your friend Kate asks to copy your homework assignment. She's been going through a lot at home lately, but cheating, even on homework, just isn't something you feel comfortable with. You . . .

   A. *tell her no loudly, and hope the teacher hears you.*

   B. *tell her no and then offer to study with her after school, when you will have time to help her.*

   C. *tell her yes, just this once. You don't want to create more problems for her.*

2. You are starting a new semester of chemistry and it's time to pick a lab partner. You've always really wanted to get to know Casey, but she is sitting a few seats away, and you don't want to come across as being pushy. You . . .

A. *ask the person next to you; she's nice enough.*

B. *signal to Casey and ask if she would like to be your partner.*

C. *wait for someone to ask you.*

3. Your best friend has been hooking up with a new boy. It's all she wants to talk about these days and you've got a lot of other things you need to focus on. You . . .

   A. *yawn, look at your watch, and hope she gets the picture that you are sick of talking about him.*

   B. *let her get her feelings off her chest now, hoping that she'll make it quick.*

   C. *tell her you need some time to focus on you, but could talk to her tomorrow night after you finish your homework.*

4. You and your friend Jen are discussing *The Hills* and suddenly realize you are completely at odds over the concept of plastic surgery. You find it pathetic. She thinks it can be empowering. When she's explaining her opinion on Heidi's breasts, you . . .

   A. *tune her out and think about something else, like how you are going to break up with her.*

   B. *listen and try to understand her point of view.*

   C. *tell her to shut up. She's an idiot and you wonder if her "hills" are real!*

5. Your friend got rejected from her top college pick and she caught you practically shouting the news across homeroom. You . . .

A. *apologize to your friend. Next time, you won't say something just to make yourself feel better.*

B. *stop, but can't resist mentioning it to an acquaintance from camp a few days later. Your friend will never know, so what's the difference?*

c. *keep spreading the news. Everyone will find out sooner or later anyway, so better that it comes from you.*

6. You and your two friends are going to the mall together. While in the car, you begin to feel like they are leaving you out of the conversation. You . . .

A. *think,* Hmmm. Maybe even numbers would be better next time.

B. *pretend that playing the role of the third wheel doesn't faze you at all. While they talk, tune out and analyze why your friendships don't ever work out.*

c. *tell them you are really hurt because they always leave you out. Ask them why they are so rude to you.*

7. You've just received an e-mail from one of the popular girls inviting you to her annual end-of-the-year-party. You've never been included before; you think:

A. *This must be some kind of a mix-up. She doesn't even know my name.*

B. *I'm a pretty cool person; glad she thinks so.*

C. *Can't wait to go, but I wonder why I made the cut. I guess it's because I'm lucky.*

8. Your friends are annoyed and accuse you of flirting with their boys. You had no idea you were "flirting" and thought you were just being friendly. You think:

A. *How interesting. Maybe they are picking up on some vibe I'm sending out. I can work on this.*

B. *What bitches. They are just jealous.*

C. *My bad! I can fix this and while I'm at it, make sure I don't do anything else to annoy them.*

9. Your best friend gets cheated on, lied to, and then dumped for the tenth time by the same guy. She never takes your advice but wants you to come over Friday night for a pity party. You have plans, so you . . .

A. *immediately drop them, saying, "Of course I'll be there. I'll bring the fudge and Kleenex."*

B. *suggest that she come with you for a change. The funny movie you are planning to see may cheer her up.*

C. *keep your plans, but end up spending most of the evening listening to her sob story via cell phone.*

10. You unwittingly commit social suicide by asking the new girl to eat lunch with you. Your friend says the long hair growing out of her chin makes her lose her appetite. You . . .

   A. tell your friend she's acting ridiculous but then eat lunch in your favorite bathroom stall until this blows over.

   B. tell your friend the friendship's off. You tell her to shut up and call you when she finds a lawnmower powerful enough to blow through her own eyebrows.

   c. shrug it off and tell her you hope she gets her appetite back by tomorrow.

Score it: Give yourself the appropriate number of points for each answer.

1. a = 2, b = 1, c = 3	**6.** a = 1, b = 2, c = 3
2. a = 2, b = 1, c = 3	**7.** a = 3, b = 1, c = 2
3. a = 2, b = 3, c = 1	**8.** a = 1, b = 3, c = 2
4. a = 2, b = 1, c = 3	**9.** a = 3, b = 1, c = 2
5. a = 1, b = 2, c = 3	**10.** a = 2, b = 3, c = 1

10-14: You are the kind of friend we all wish we had. You know who you are, and you appreciate who your friends are and want them to be happy. You don't stoop to their level when they are low, but rather raise them to yours. You know when you're right and you know when you're wrong—but you don't make too much of either. If you're not careful, your phone will never stop ringing!

15-25: You are well on your way to finding balance in friendship, because balance is really the key to having friendships that work for everybody. You *are pretty honest with your friends, but please resist the temptation to fix them or wallow in their occasional self-pity. Worry less about letting them down, and more about letting yourself down.*

26-30: *Drama queen, it doesn't always have to be like this. Don't host the pity party every time your friend gets dumped and don't host her lynching every time your feelings get hurt. Try to keep your thoughts—even in the most dramatic made-for-TV-movie situations—focused on the outcome you want. Do you want this to blow up into a huge thing? Or do you just want to be heard?*

This Is the Deal

Maybe you have an older sister or cousin who filled you in on the social scene in your new school. She gave you all sorts of pearls of "wisdom" about navigating the scene. But as you walk through the doors on the first day, your hopes have been extinguished by the realization that school can be a social mine field and you are in danger of becoming a future contestant on *Dancing with the Stars*. Tight cliques of girls roam the hallways like they are on border patrol, able to shoot down unsuspecting victims with a look of the evil eye. And if you make the mistake of *talking* to one of the older boys, you might as well just tape a bull's-eye on your back. To make matters worse, later that week it comes out that your crush from the summer wants to hook up with your best friend. And your neighbor since second grade has changed into someone you hardly recognize (in part due to an overzealous application of self-tanner). And WHERE are you supposed to sit at lunch anyway? You can't help but think back to the good old days, before there was so much drama . . . when everyone just hung out together.

News flash. Everyone, including the Border Patrol, is trying to figure out who their friends are and how they fit in. Everyone is changing quickly, and even the most popular girls are feeling out of sorts. Some kids may even be dealing with serious home life issues, which can explain some negative behavior that has more to do with them than you.

So remember that not everyone is looking at you. Wave good-bye to your imaginary audience, they were never there. These will be great years—provided you keep that Friend Energy flowing in the direction you want.

Try to think about your social life as yet another required course on your busy schedule. The good news is that you are in charge of the curriculum. You define what you want out of your social life and focus on it, feel good about it, and make sure your actions line up with it. You can focus on finding friends you can be yourself around. You can focus on being popular. We suggest you focus on the feeling you are looking for. What will having better friends bring you?

Reading your thoughts and feelings as you interact with others will be your only assignment. There is only one grade . . . and that is how good you feel about yourself. Hey, this could be fun.

The key is, once you get in the flow, you will be able to apply what you've learned everywhere in life. And later on, when you are in college, or working, or President . . . you'll be clicking send on all sorts of cool vibes, bringing all sorts of cool people into your social circle. That's because the very same issues you are dealing with now will repeat over and over for the rest of your life.

TO: **Click!**
FROM: **Not So G-L-A-M-O-R-O-U-S**
RE: **Help!**

. . . .

Monika is the richest and most popular girl in my grade. Her designer bag collection is big enough to fill both Mary-Kate's and Ashley's closets. She has all the best clothes and always has the best parties. Lately Monika has been asking my two best friends to do stuff with her (like go to her parents' beach house, take a limo to go shopping in the city, or use her dad's box seats for an amazing concert). I am never invited. Afterward, Monika goes out of her way to tell me what a great time they had. I feel like she wants me to feel left out. And she brags about all her Balenciaga bags all the time, knowing that my family barely makes ends meet. This is a girl who has everything. Why is she being so mean?

↩ **Reply:**

. . . .

Fergie may describe Monika as flying first class up in the sky, but we would call this behavior Ludacris! We know it's hard to hear this, but despite the clothes, the beach house, the limo into the city, the parties, and the box seats, Monika is just another girl who feels down in the dumps about herself. Her issues—and her shoes—may differ from yours, but when you get to the heart of it, Monika is quite miserable. We can speculate that perhaps her parents were too busy to give her the love she craved and, out of guilt, pimped her ride with stuff. Fast forward to the present, and that's how Monika feels better . . . prancing around in her Jimmy Choos. And when all that stuff isn't enough to get Monika over the feeling-good hump, she'll just pick on others to make them feel as bad as she does. (Think Macaulay Culkin in *Richie Rich.*)

Before you play the V-card and pack your bags for Blamingham, let's think about what you really want. How about feeling like you have control? How about knowing that her having stuff doesn't take anything away from you? Decide that you are no longer the victim. The best thing to do is to start preparing for your next close encounter with Monika. Your goal is to feel good about yourself, without stooping to her level and being cruel.

It wouldn't hurt to *get some action* here. The next time she says something mean, have some pre-scripted responses in your back pocket. If she starts bragging about her new bling, you can say something like, "I am thrilled for you." If she starts being flat-out mean, you could ask in your calmest voice, "Is something going on with you?" and leave it at that. The key is for you to feel like you have the reins. E-vite: *I'm cool with or without all that stuff.* RSVP: *Yes.*

Another way to feel better is to focus on the friends you already have. You have other people to hang out with. Foster these friendships and have a good time. Your friends will come back to you, probably with Monika in tow.

. . . .

School's over and my crush, Pablo, just hosted THE graduation party. Pablo's
parents went all out. Caterer, DJ, waitstaff in white gloves . . . Everyone said it was
going to be a party to be remembered. After we'd been dancing for hours, everyone
was getting kind of crazy. I was having a blast on the dance floor and pretty soon a
crowd had gathered in a circle and started chanting "Flip her, flip her, flip her."

Pablo and his friends grabbed me and yelled, "One . . . Two . . . Three!" I
screamed and struggled (which totally freaked Pablo out). That's how I ended up
stuck upside down, mid-flip, with my legs kicking in the air. My dress was over my
head, which meant my old Barbie Princess underwear was on display for all to see
. . . teachers, aunts, uncles, sophomores, juniors, seniors this year's and last year's
championship soccer team.

Pablo got a good look and let me drop to the ground awkwardly, and I
struggled to pull my dress down and assess the damage. Pablo asked if I was okay
and assured me that barely anyone saw. But no one would make eye contact with
me, except Pablo's older cousin Sebastian, who smiled with a glazed, perverted
look in his eye.

I ran outside to find my friends and get it together . . . That's when I bumped
into Pablo's mom coming out of the bathroom. "Oh, sweetheart . . . you must be
soooo humiliated . . . Are you okay?"

↺ **Reply:**

. . . .

Yes . . . this will be a party to remember! Let's use Photoshop to make
sure we remember it the way we want to remember it. Although you

can't erase what happened, you can frame it in a way that makes you feel a little better. Let's give it a try.

We don't like feeling humiliated, so let's pick the "funny" border instead. We'll look at the big picture, adjust the brightness and contrast, and crop some things out.

Look at the Big Picture: What is going on here? Let's begin with the fact that there is no way everyone at the party saw your little show. People are always wrapped up in their own drama. For those who got a glimpse, a little flash o' Barbie never hurt anyone. Your brief moment under the lights didn't last more than a few seconds. Plus it wasn't even captured on film, so you can be grateful for that. What's more, half the people at that party probably have a pair of goofy underwear anyway. And you apparently look cute with Barbie on your butt. Can we focus on that?

Crop out Sebastian's skeevy look. He was most likely drunk and probably didn't know he was doing it. Let's not take him too seriously.

Brightness: Let's notice how polite and sensitive Pablo and even his mom were about the incident. Wow. Very cool of them. You picked well.

Can you enlarge the funny part of this picture? Really, if you wanted to be a stand-up comic, you would have enough material for your first gig and then some. Can you laugh about it? Maybe someday down the road, you will be able to use it in a book you write.

Reduce red eye: Let's put a stop to those tears. Unless they are tears of laughter.

· ·

I have this new friend Mindy who is really fun and we have such a great time together. A few weeks ago I started spending a lot of time with this guy Ed. When I told Mindy, she seemed so happy for me at first. But then I discovered that she is spreading lies that I hooked up with Ed and that I am a slut. I am shocked because Mindy knows the truth (that we haven't), and she is supposed to be my friend. I am so embarrassed to go to school, but defending myself makes it look like she is right.

↩ **Reply:**
· ·

Poor Mindy. Not only is she a first-class bitch, but she is obviously desperate. She wants to be popular so badly that she has in effect thrown you under a bus to get there. She had a morsel of information. She tossed it to the dogs. It whetted their appetite and they wanted more, more, more! She was there to give it to them and it felt great!

Gossip gives the gossiper such a feeling of power. They are up onstage and a hushed audience is hanging on their every word. Why not embellish, especially when you know the high is so short-lived? Okay, we are done with doing the Dr. Phil on Mindy.

The most important thing for you to do is take that V-card you were about to play, and put it back in your pocket. You are not going to be a victim of gossip. *Get some action* by confronting Mindy with the basic "You know this is not true, why are you saying it?" and then disengage from this discussion. Everyone knows you have one story and she has another and everyone is going to make up her own mind about it. But the more you keep focusing on it, the more conversation and speculation will grow around it. If you spend all your time stewing and talking about *everyone says I hooked up with Ed and I can't believe it,* the E-vite reads: *Everyone says I hooked up with Ed.* RSVP: *Yes.* They'll keep saying it. Let it die, know who you are, and ditch Mindy today.

· ·

My neighbor Julie was my best friend in elementary and middle school. Our moms are best friends and we shared clothes for years until I grew five inches taller than her. Last summer we spent every single day together. We were so excited about starting high school, we planned our outfits for the first day back in July. A week into high school, she started hanging out with a bunch of sophomores and now she acts like she doesn't even know me. I've lost my best friend and I can't even tell her how angry I am because she ignores me!

↩ **Reply:**

· ·

Julie is not quite (oh, how do we put this?) there yet. She does not know who she is, and she is not looking to herself for guidance. She is in a chameleon phase, taking on the exact color of whatever is passing by. She is so worried about who she is going to end up being in high school (a nerd? a jock? popular?) that she is willing to ditch you any time it seems like a better deal may be coming along.

So what to do? Let's shift our focus away from Julie's identity crisis. Get out your journal and *write your story.* Start writing about what you want. You probably want your friendship with Julie back and probably want to feel like you fit in somewhere in high school too. Can you write about how it's going to be? Can you imagine how it will be to feel secure in your group of friends? If this ordeal with Julie has taught you anything, it's how much you want to feel like you are secure in your friendships. Can you turn your attention to the friends that are not treating you like last season's sale rack? Try to click send on: *I am going to have great friendships in high school.*

TO: **Click!**
FROM: **Clean and Sober**
RE: **Help!**
· ·

I am going to a party this weekend. I was getting really excited about it, talking with my friends about where we were going to get dressed, how we were going to get there, etc. Then one of my friends started talking about how her brother was going to score some pot for the party. I know there are going to be lots of drugs there. I am not into that at all, but I really want to go to the party anyway. And I don't want to come across as a goody-goody.

↺ **Reply:**
· ·

We've been there and done that. There are lots of tricks to seem cool while staying true to your gut. You can say, "Yeah, I'd really love to sniff that stuff up my nose, but I'm having rhinoplasty tomorrow." Or, this is a good one: "Sure, I'd love to take one of those little pills and find myself naked with a stranger and a potential spinal cord injury, but I have a little tummy ache."

special topics: let's focus

Okay, so that's ridiculous, right? If you've made up your mind not to do something, you have to just stick to it. And be real about it. Being cool is not about doing what your friends are doing, or acting however cool is manifesting itself in the media. True cool comes from knowing who you are and clicking send on the E-vites that really represent what you want. Cool is Angelina Jolie, stepping out of Hollywood and into Africa. And as much as it pains us to say this, cool is Regina George in *Mean Girls*. Remember when Janis cut nipple holes in her tank top? She just shrugged, wore it anyway, and started a trend. Cool is knowing who you are. Cool is just being authentic.

So take a second to pat yourself on the back for knowing not only what you are getting yourself into but how you feel about it. Bust out with something crazy like "no thanks" or "nope, not for me." Trust us, people don't really want to share their drugs anyway. Stay true, don't feel like you need to explain your position. You are clicking send on so many good things: *I am me. I respect me. I am cool.* RSVP: Yes. You are.

TO: Click!
FROM: Out of the Loop
RE: Help!
. . . .

I have a really tight group of eight friends, and we do everything together. Last month, I went away for spring break with my family and they were all home. When I got back I heard about all that had happened while I was gone and it sounded really fun. I felt left out but blew it off. But they are still talking about this big week I missed and telling inside jokes and saying, "Don't worry about it, you wouldn't get it." I feel like I've lost my spot in the group.

Don't worry, your friends are just drunk on the power of the group. They are feeling so bonded and secure in their enjoyment of Whatever Happened During the Big Week that they don't want you to kill their buzz. They'll sober up in time to have a great time with you soon. But in the meantime don't go all desperate on them. Don't do the "Guys! Tell me! I feel so left out!!!" It just gives fuel to the power of this (whatever!) story and more attention to the fact that you missed it. Hang back and let this one blow over. E-vite: *I'm still secure.*

e-vite rewrite

CURRENT E-VITE	E-VITE REWRITE
I don't have any friends.	*I know I can make friends; I've done it before. It was easiest when I was just being myself.*
The cool girls ignore me.	*There are plenty of people who know what a cool person I am.*
All my friends are total backstabbers; one day we're bad-mouthing Sonia, and the next they are all bad-mouthing me with Sonia!	*There are lots of people I can trust. I don't have to gossip; we have other things we can talk about.*
I can't take the pressure I feel from my friends to do things I don't want to do.	*I am confident enough in myself to make my own decisions and feel good about them.*
My best friend dumped me for a cooler crowd. I am devastated.	*I really want to have good friends who I can count on. I know that I will attract these kinds of people.*

me, myself, and my body—can't we be friends again?

Test Your Body Energy

1. You forgot to reapply your sunblock and got a sunburn. You think:

   A. *I'm such an idiot. I see melanoma in my future. Immediately start Googling melanoma survival rates.*

   B. *I could have been better about putting on sunblock. I'll make sure I do better next time.*

   C. *Can't do anything about it now. As the saying goes . . . what can go wrong, will go wrong.*

2. You've been working hard at losing weight and you lost four pounds. You think:

A. *It's probably just water weight and I will gain it right back after dinner.*

B. *This diet is like magic. But I still can't fit into my little sister's jeans.*

C. *My hard work is really showing. I feel amazing and healthy and strong and hot hot hot.*

3. You've been great about getting exercise but you've fallen off the wagon for the past few weeks. You think:

A. *I know I always feel better when I exercise. Tonight I'll get new music for my iPod and tomorrow I'm going to the gym.*

B. *I've been so lazy! I am definitely going to try to run everyday after school this week.*

C. *There is never enough time in the day. If I wasn't so busy, I could work out more.*

4. You are wearing your new pair of Jack Rogers and your friend comments on how ugly your toes are. You . . .

A. *agree. But unlike her, at least you get pedicures. Dr. Scholl won't be calling her anytime soon.*

B. *are pissed! It's not your fault that ugly feet are the family curse.*

C. *think hammer toes aren't so bad and at least they are fungus- and odor-free!*

5. The goalie on the opposing soccer team blocked your shot. You think:

A. *I didn't think fast enough. I should have passed the ball to Anne.*

B. *She's good but if I shoot more to her left, I think I'll score.*

C. *Hopefully, our defense will keep them from scoring. Ever since my knee injury, I haven't been very reliable.*

6. You have a bad cold. You think:

A. *Cold and flu season is such a bummer! It's like this year after year.*

B. *I guess everyone gets colds now and then. I just can't believe I forgot to use Purel after I babysat for those sick kids last week.*

C. *Time to take it easy. Even rock stars give it a rest every once in a while.*

7. You hurt your ankle hiking with your friends. The doctor thinks it's just a sprain. You think:

A. *I was looking forward to that ski trip we all planned. I probably won't be better by then, so I won't get my hopes up.*

B. *I'm still nervous it might be broken. Maybe we should get a fifth opinion.*

C. *Last time I had a sprained ankle, it healed in a week. I am so looking forward to going on that ski trip in a few months.*

8. You rarely get acne, but this morning you have a huge zit on your chin. You . . .

A. *cover it up and move on.*

B. *run to the dermatologist in tears.*

C. *laugh it off, but point it out to everyone and anyone who you talk to.*

9. You know you get really bad cramps and are extremely moody around your period, so you . . .

A. *laugh with your friends about it; they can relate!*

B. *get pissed at your mom because you probably inherited the "PMS" gene from her.*

C. *pretend it's not a big deal . . . until you lose your temper at your cat.*

10. You cut out a picture in a magazine of the perfect mane of hair. When your hairdresser fails to get it right on you, you . . .

A. *start to cry and wonder why you ever bothered trying.*

B. *realize your pal Alica has similar hair to yours. Hers always looks good, and you make a mental note to ask where she goes.*

C. *smile and say thanks, but don't leave a tip. Maybe she'll learn a lesson and go back to beauty school.*

Score it: Give yourself the appropriate number of points for each answer.

1. a = 3, b = 1, c = 2   **6.** a = 3, b = 2, c = 1

2. a = 3, b = 2, c = 1   **7.** a = 2, b = 3, c = 1

3. a = 1, b =2, c = 3   **8.** a = 1, b = 3, c = 2

4. a = 2, b = 3, c = 1   **9.** a = 1, b = 3, c = 2

5. a = 3, b = 1, c = 2   .   **10.** a = 3, b = 1, c = 2

10-14: *You feel good about how you look, but most of all you feel good about who you are. You've called a truce with yourself and if your hair's not working and your face is bursting, you take it in stride. You are clicking send on true beauty.*

15-25: *Not bad, hottie. You feel pretty good about how you look and feel, although you are still taking it a bit seriously. You have a tendency to obsess a bit and your overzealous approach may have you clicking send on lukewarm. Trust your first gut reaction and don't overthink things.*

26-30: *For Pete's sake, would you lighten up a little? Don't make a mountain out of a pimple. Shift that focus away from what's bothering you, because you are attracting an avalanche of "I feel crappy" to crash on your doorstep.*

This Is the Deal

It's hard to remember when it started. One day you just felt totally let down by your body. She'd been like a good friend, fun to bury in the sand, fun to swing on a tree limb with. And then one day you noticed the betrayal. When did my thighs start spreading out like that every time I sit down? Is that a mustache growing over my lip? When did I grow into such a conspicuous giant that I bump my head on Exit signs? And, BTW, thanks so much for all this, but where are my boobs?

And this estranged friend feels bad too. She's sad that you no longer feel comfortable with her. She misses the days when you sat cross-legged in a bathing suit building a sand castle. But, missy, she has a bone to pick with you, too. Why did you cut me down to five hundred calories a day on Wednesday, and then shove McDonald's down my throat all day Thursday? And what was that stuff you kept drinking on Friday night to such excess that I actually had to vomit to save myself from it? And why do you keep TALKING about me that way? Can't we be friends again?

The answer is yes, you are going to have to make up. Unlike friends who come in different shapes and sizes and can be replaced, this bod comes in just that one shape and one size and she's all yours. Make the best of her, treat her well. Stop talking about her behind her back, she hears you.

Your beefs with your body are standing in the way of so much happiness in your life. Your body is available (desperate even!) to provide you with a lifetime of pleasure. So let's see if we can tackle a few complaints and start sending better E-vites about the old gal.

special topics: let's focus

→ *List your five favorite things about your body.*

SEND			_ □ X
TO:	The Universe		
FROM:	Trying to Make Peace		
CC:	The Whole World		
RE:	What I like about my body		

TO: **Click!**
FROM: **Weight Warrior**
RE: **Help!**

I am always struggling with my weight. All I want is to look thin and feel good in jeans or a bathing suit. I have tried every diet, and nothing works. I even tried to cut my calories to 750 a day and ended up still gaining weight. I have no self-control.

↺ Reply:

. . . .

We think the only thing in the world that will make you fat faster than cheesecake is your crazy diet. Sure, you have the Focus Factor busily at work, but you are focusing on the wrong thing. When you go on a diet, you are suddenly focused on two things—how fat you feel, and food. You carefully plan out what you are going to eat all day, you measure and weigh your portions. Suddenly, you're starving and who knew the Domino's guy delivered at 10 a.m.? E-vite: *Feeling fat and starving.* RSVP: *Yes.*

Add this to your diet—*feeling good about what you want.* You probably want to feel healthy and confident. Going out and doing something fun and wearing something that makes you feel good sends this E-vite: *I feel great about myself.* RSVP: *Yes.* Chances are if you feel great, you probably won't find yourself polishing off a box of Krispy Kremes in the dark.

Instead of making a big chore out of your carefully planned food and exercise regimen, think of how fun it would be to go for a bike ride. Maybe you can make a detour past hot George Manning's house on the way. If it's fun, you are probably going to keep doing more of it. This is a good time to *Get Some Action.* Find healthy foods that you like to eat and ways to be active that are fun for you. If healthy feels good, you'll be inviting in more of it. E-vite: *I feel healthy.* If you are sitting at home staring at the clock and waiting for your next carrot stick, you are more likely to end up with your nose in a box of Girl Scout cookies.

I was born with a long birthmark on my butt. I never really focused on it before, but all of sudden a kid at the pool noticed it and said that it looked like a banana. Now all the kids are calling me Monkey Girl. I feel so gross about it and I'm afraid to get up without wrapping a towel around my butt.

↺ **Reply:**

Stop swinging through the vines for a second and listen to your E-vite. You are clicking send on: *Insecurity and ugliness.* This birthmark is a unique part of who you are. Take off that cover up and dive back in to your summer.

Try to rewrite your E-vite by thinking of the things that make you feel beautiful. You weren't so focused on this before someone pointed it out, so don't start clicking send on their E-vites. Refocus on the things you do like about yourself. What kind of legs are under that birthmark anyway? What about your eyes? Your hair? Don't let someone's offhanded comment keep you from enjoying your vacation.

Why not Photoshop this? Can you make that birthmark look slightly less like a banana and more like a boomerang? If nothing else, it'll be a reminder of the Focus Factor every time you see it.

· ·

I found a picture of myself in a bathing suit from last summer. OMG, I looked like a whale. I had no idea I'd gotten so chunks. My sister told me to put the picture up on the refrigerator so that I'd be motivated to eat healthy. I thought visualization stuff was supposed to help! This didn't work at all. Why not?

↺ **Reply:**

· ·

Lucky for you, we don't actually have a dunce cap. Have you heard anything we've said? That picture is up there reminding you of how you don't want to feel. You click send on what you don't want every time you hit the fridge. E-vite: *Fat in a bathing suit.* RSVP: *Yes.* Now go to the back of the class.

To refresh your memory, *visualize your course* and imagine your body looking the way you want it to. Feel how strong and energetic you are. See yourself as you want to be.

TO: **Click!**

FROM: **Fashion Victim**

RE: **Help!**

· ·

Every time I go clothes shopping I feel like there are too many things about myself that I need to change. I'm short-waisted and have broad shoulders and nothing ever seems to fit.

The last time we went shopping, we started to get dizzy from all the choices. Nobody looks perfect in every style, and that's why the fashion industry makes so many different things. When you wear something that you don't feel comfortable in just because it's what your friends are wearing or because it looks great on a seven-foot model, your E-vite is: *I look ridiculous.*

There are clothes out there that will look great on you, no matter what your body type. Take a little time and look at your favorite clothes in your closet. How high do the jeans come? Where's the waist on that minidress that hits you in exactly the right spot? Shop with an eye for what will look great on you. Chances are that the seven-foot model you've been comparing yourself to wouldn't look as good in your favorite minidress as you do. Your best style will be your own style anyway. If you don't believe us, go to Dove.com. Your new E-vite is: *Check me out!*

TO: **Click!**
FROM: **Frustrated Athlete**
RE: **Help!**

I really wanted to start on the volleyball team this year. I was positioned to start, but this new girl transferred in to my school who is about a foot taller than I am and who is rumored to be really good. Everyone knows that tall people make better volleyball players. It's so unfair. I am screwed because of my short, stubby legs. Since it is impossible that I will ever have jumps like hers, why bother trying?

↺ Reply:

∙∙∙

Your E-vite reads like a bad movie: *Short People Can't Jump*. It's time to archive your beliefs about what makes someone a good athlete and save over the old file with a new belief. We tend to download lots of myths about things, without thinking. Just because the majority of people believe something doesn't automatically make it true. Usually, once someone dispels the myth, other people follow suit. Sure, maybe some tall people are good at volleyball, but that doesn't mean all tall people make better volleyball players than you.

We'd like to see you on the team, so let's rewrite your E-vite before you literally throw in the towel. First of all, you know you are good at volleyball. You have played for years. Your "short, stubby" legs are actually muscular and have given you strength in the past. Show them some gratitude. The reality is that there is room for more than just one new starter. Try to click send on: *I am a good volleyball player and I am qualified to start.* When you can really feel it, click send and you are well on your way.

Have you ever heard the story about the four-minute mile? Until 1954, it was a commonly held belief that is was impossible for a person to run a mile in less than four minutes. People truly focused on this impossibility (remember they had no cable TV, so what else could they do?), studied it, and concluded that the structure of the human body could not, would not ever break the four-minute-mile barrier. They believed this until Roger Bannister came along and decided that this made no sense. Bannister thought that the barrier was all psychological, and that the belief in the barrier was a self-

special topics: let's focus

fulfilling prophecy. He ran the four-minute mile in three minutes and 59.4 seconds. The world was stunned. But the most interesting thing about this story is that, after he broke the four-minute barrier, sixteen other runners also broke it within three years. It was as if seeing Bannister do it had reversed a belief and opened up a whole new kind of E-vite: *This can be done.* RSVP: *Yes.*

Or think of Maria Sharapova. Despite the fact that women tennis players did not historically make as much money as men, she did not roll over and accept the commonly held belief. No . . . instead, Maria, the business-savvy girl she is, said, "Show me the money." Today, Sharapova is one of the highest-paid athletes in the world—higher than many of her male counterparts in the tennis world. Ad-In for Sharapova. See where a little thinking outside the "service box" can get you? E-vite: *Just do it!* RSVP: *Ka-ching!*

e-vite rewrite

CURRENT E-VITE	E-VITE REWRITE
I am so fat! Why did I eat all those donuts? I hate myself!	*I am grateful for my health. I know that I can make better food choices.*
I have no boobs—it's totally unfair.	*It'll be fun to see what my body looks like when I'm totally developed. But, whatever. Lots of supermodels are totally flat chested and look great.*
I am so uncoordinated, gym is totally humiliating.	*I enjoy walking and running outside and have done just fine in track and field.*
I am cursed with a short, squat body.	*I am short and I feel beautiful.*

the daily grind

Pop Quiz: Test Your School/ Sports/Extras Energy

1. You received a really good grade on your pop quiz. You think:

   A. *I sure am smart!*

   B. *Thank God the teacher asked the right questions.*

   C. *I guess I picked the right day to tune in!*

2. You fall asleep in English class and wake up drooling. You think:

   A. *Live and learn. I won't watch an entire season of* Laguna Beach *on a school night again.*

   B. *At least I didn't get caught snoring. . . . But you have to admit, this situation is soooo embarrassing.*

   C. *I am a lousy student. What is wrong with me?*

3. You raise your hand and your teacher doesn't call on you.
You . . .

   A. *wave your hand like crazy the next time the teacher asks a question. You know the right answer and need to be heard.*

   B. *decide the guy behind you had his hand raised first. Your teacher needs to give everyone a turn.*

   C. *try not to focus on it, but end up dwelling on the incident the rest of the day.*

4. You don't finish your exam on time. You think:

   A. *Bummer. Maybe I can get some help getting organized.*

   B. *I am such an idiot. I'll probably fail.*

   C. *Nothing I can do about it now. Why did I forget to wear my watch?*

5. Your teacher cuts you off before you finish answering a question.
You . . .

   A. *realize that he's probably just having a bad day, but he didn't have to be so rude.*

   B. *laugh at the situation. There were only ten minutes left in class, he had to keep moving.*

   C. *clear your throat and say loudly, "Excuse me, what I was trying to say was . . ."*

6. You really want to join the chorus. At tryouts you . . .

   A. *compare your voice to the other girls and pray the musical director doesn't force you to sing a high C.*

   B. *think about how much fun you'll have when you make the chorus.*

   C. *do your proper breathing exercises, while thinking how much it would suck if you tripped and fell off the stage during your audition.*

7. You never seem to make your free throws. You think:

   A. *If I shoot for just a few minutes after each practice, I'll get better.*

   B. *Everyone has slumps now and then. I just have a few more than most people.*

   C. *I am really letting my team down. I am sure I will be benched soon.*

8. You tried out for the soccer team and didn't make the cut. You . . .

   A. *wallow in your sorrows for the next week. You can't seem to catch a break.*

   B. *think,* This gives me time to focus on other things this fall. I've always wanted to try yoga.

   C. *congratulate your friend for making the team and then have her critique your soccer skills. Did she ever notice how slow you are?*

9. You just won the election for class president. You . . .

   A. *jump up and down for joy. You really are so excited.*

   B. *think it was a fluke. Shhh. . . . Someone should demand a recount.*

   C. *feel great but kind of dread all the extra work it's going to be.*

10. You open your final exam only to realize you have no idea as to how to answer the first question. You . . .

   A. *think,* I'm so screwed.

   B. *do the other problems first. You can come back to that question later.*

   C. *do the other problems first while wondering why you forgot to study something so important.*

Score it: Give yourself the appropriate number of points for each answer.

1. a = 1, b = 3, c = 2	**6.** a = 3, b = 1, c = 2
2. a = 1, b = 2, c = 3	**7.** a = 1, b = 2, c = 3
3. a = 3, b =1, c = 2	**8.** a = 3, b = 1, c = 2
4. a = 1, b = 3, c = 2	**9.** a = 1, b = 3, c = 2
5. a = 2, b = 1, c = 3	**10.** a = 3, b = 1, c = 2

10-14: *Royal Highness of High School, you are seated comfortably on your throne. You are optimistic and clicking send on* I am having a great time even when things aren't perfect. *You are your own best cheerleader. You take credit when things go your way and responsibility when they don't.*

15-25: *Focus just a little harder and you'll be on that throne in no time. You just need to keep your eye on what you want. It's as if you are at the finish line and then self-doubt makes you take two giant steps back before you cross it.*

26-30: *How can we put this? There is only one thing keeping you from rocking your school: you. You've got to get out of your own way and quit clicking send on anger and blame. The truth is that no one's out to get you, they're all too worried about what they want. Take their clue and focus. You did something great? Cheer yourself. You screwed up? Learn from it. The reason you think everyone is so hard on you is that you are so hard on yourself. E-vite all day long:* Hard on me. *RSVP:* Yes.

This Is the Deal

Besides your parents, the one thing that stands between you and a good time is your schoolwork. And we don't just mean your history paper. Schoolwork used to be a bunch of kids in a little red schoolhouse learning their ABCs and enough math so that they could one day run Ye Olde Country Store. No longer. Your schoolwork is tests and quizzes and sports teams and student council and band and the Chinese club. The real reason you are the first generation to have electronic organizers is that you are the first generation to need them.

And yet. Part of you loves it. If school was just hanging out in the hallways all day checking out the latest fashion victim, it would get pretty boring. While some things you are learning are making you wish for a quick death (anyone read *Beowulf*? Okay, we're on the same page), other things you can really sink your teeth into, like *The Outsiders.* The problem is that there's too much to do and often you are so freaked out and overwhelmed that your E-vites are: *Panic and dread.* You'll miss all the good stuff.

Here's a trick for you that will prove to be true during these years and beyond: Be where you are. When you are in science lab and you are going over every experiment that is going to be on next week's test, don't space out and think about Friday night's soccer game. If you dedicate the hour to the science lab, you won't have to relearn it all on your own later and miss the soccer game on Friday. Or switch it around. What if you daydreamed about the soccer game in science class, missed the review, and then ended up so stressed out that you were actually flipping though your science text during the soccer game. Just a little unsolicited advice for school and life.

Take everything bit by bit, course by course. Your E-vites will read: *Confident and capable.* And should you screw it all up royally (don't click send but it's a possibility), take it in stride and move on.

TO: **Click!**
FROM: **Quitter?**
RE: **Help!**
· ·

I signed up to be photography editor of the yearbook because I love to take pictures and thought it would be cool and would look good on my college applications. It's been two months and I'm totally burned out. It's so much more work than I thought it was going to be. I've already missed two deadlines! I think the editor-in-chief is going to make me quit.

· ·

Life is all about choices, and you probably made three or four before you got out of bed this morning. But the most important place to start is—here we go again—figuring out what you really want. Our guess is that since you love photography, you don't really want to have to quit. And the fact that you've been made photography editor means that you have a talent for this kind of thing. Your current E-vite reads: *I am overwhelmed and failing.* But at the end of the day do you want Photography Editor under your picture and memories to last a lifetime?

The second piece of the puzzle, after you've figured out what you want, is to make sure that your energy is grounded so that you can focus on what you want without getting overwhelmed. Turn to the back of this book and look at your journal. How have you organized your time? Make a list of the steps you need to take to make the next deadline and write in when you are going to do them. Make sure you've budgeted enough time to accomplish each task. We recommend breaking things down into small chunks. As you make small accomplishments, you'll be sending new E-vites that read: *I can do this.* You will feel more and more competent as you check things off your list.

TO: **Click!**
FROM: **Not Dealing**
RE: **Help!**

· ·

I have so many things in my life that I just don't want to deal with. I have a term paper to write and I can think of about a thousand things I'd rather be doing right now. If I'm supposed to feel good and know what I want, can't I just blow this stuff off? I definitely do not want to write this paper. But I feel like I have no choice.

You do have a choice about writing this paper. You can either write the paper or fail English. As much as you hate the idea of having to dive headfirst into a term paper about a bunch of dead kings, you do like the idea of passing English and graduating from high school. There are always going to be things in your reality that you don't want to deal with. You could choose to blow off getting the oil changed in your car, but you are sort of attached to having something to drive.

The true magic key to living a life of pure bliss is to focus on all the things you love to do, while finding things to love in all the things you have to do. (Did that sound like a country song? Sorry.) And by "have to do," we mean things you have chosen to do because you like the things that come along with them. If you hate your job washing dishes at the local diner, but you love that your weekly paycheck's getting you closer to that awesome BCBG dress, then suck it up. Make it fun, find some cute fry cook to flirt with, and *get some 'tude* about having this job at all. Bitching about it will make a situation you have chosen to stick out even more miserable. The E-vite can read: *Sunny day, BCBG dress.* Or it can read: *This sucks.*

TO: **Click!**
FROM: **Victimizo**
RE: **Help!**

My Spanish teacher has a personal vendetta against me. She criticizes everything I do and grades my papers harder than everyone else's. I'm worried it's going to ruin my grade.

. . . .

Tough one. Maybe you look exactly like the girl who stole her boyfriend in high school. Whatever it is, you'll probably never know. But what we do know is that as long as you have it in your head that she hates you, you will probably continue to create situations that irritate her. It's just like when you are around that friend who thinks you are hysterical, and suddenly you are channeling Chris Rock.

You need to shift your focus away from how you think she feels. Focus on how you want her to see you. And then just focus on your Spanish homework. You probably don't want to go to the movies with her on Saturday night anyway. What you really want is to do well in Spanish and feel fairly treated. Focus there.

TO: **Click!**
FROM: **Scholastic Disaster**
RE: **Help!**

. . . .

Last year I had a C– average, and that's just because my algebra teacher took pity on me. I want to get better grades so badly that I even stay up most nights way past midnight trying to study. It's not fair that some kids can just phone in a B without even trying. It's not my fault if school doesn't come easily to me. My mom says that she and my dad both had a really hard time in school too. It's just the way we are. I feel like giving up.

. . . .

It sounds like you are fighting an uphill battle. School is hard, life's not fair, and you are genetically programmed to flunk. School really can be hard, but you've been struggling for so long that you have been spending years clicking send on: *I'm a terrible student.* That E-vite brings fear of school, a cloudy mind, and plenty of frustration to the party. No wonder you're discouraged. Put down that V-card you're about to play and let's get a new party started.

The first thing to do is rewrite those E-vites. How about: *It'll feel so good to do better in school* or *Just because my parents weren't good students doesn't mean I am destined to follow in their footsteps.* We bet there are lots of things you *are* good at. Spend some time thinking about those things. Now let's take it one step further. Can you remember a time where you felt like you did well on something in school? Feel free to time travel . . . it can be your second grade pinch pot or your fourth grade homework assignment . . . we're just looking for a feeling here. Now come back to the present and imagine how much better a C average would feel. Then can you get to a B-? Trying to leap from where you are to the honor roll would be too frustrating. You want to feel good as you shift your energy, not discouraged.

Send all the great E-vites you want, but you are also going to have to meet the Universe halfway here. In order to get yourself unstuck from this feeling of helplessness, we recommend that you *get some action.* You may be burning the midnight oil studying harder than anyone in your grade, but are you studying efficiently? Learning is not always about hours spent staring at the material; rather, it's often about grasping a concept and being able to think clearly about it. Maybe you need to talk to your teachers to make sure you understand their lesson plans as well as their expectations.

We'd also like you to *get grounded*. How can you manage your busy schedule if you are constantly pulling all-nighters? Your lack of sleep may be zapping your energy, making it difficult to focus while you are in class. Waking up on the wrong side of the bed, your wheels spinning, leads to a day filled with more of the same. Maybe you could rearrange your schedule to begin studying earlier in the evening. You may want to begin with the subjects that require the most concentration, and save the easier assignments for later. When you talk to your teacher, we suggest you also ask for advice in structuring your schedule and managing your time and energy more effectively.

Are you feeling a little better yet? Just for fun . . . here's a Pop Quiz: If we offered you two pairs of $150 Paige jeans for $100, would you think that was a good deal? Great job! You're clicking send on: *Math Whiz* already.

TO: **Click!**
FROM: **Out in Left Field**
RE: **Help!**
. . . .

Softball is probably the most important thing in my life. I am on my school team in the spring and practice all summer and in the off-season. My real strength is pitching, and I know that I am one of the best pitchers on my team. The problem is that one of my teammates is my coach's niece. He totally favors her and plays

her as our starting pitcher at every game. She's not half as committed to the
game as I am and, as a pitcher, I think she's really unpredictable. How can I make
him see that he's being totally unfair?

↺ **Reply:**

. . . .

It's a bummer not to feel acknowledged for your hard work. But the
E-vite you are sending is hitting the Universe loud and clear: *It's not
fair!* Keep focusing on how unfair this is and you might find yourself
winning the team's Most Likely to Have a Crappy Attitude award.

Don't strike out. Instead, let's get in sync with your goal—to get
off the bench. First of all, start rewriting your E-vites. Shift your focus
away from the drama and back to where it was when you loved the
game, namely on your skills. Click send on: *I know I am a great pitcher. I
love this game.* RSVP: *Yes.* Now try to *visualize your course.* Just think how
calm you'll feel consistently getting the ball over the plate and striking
out batters. Imagine catching a pop-up and throwing the runner out
at second. Now envision your turn at the plate and hear the crack of
the ball on your bat. You hit a double! Now let's *get some action.* Go to
practice and work hard and think about how great it's going to be when
you are chosen to start at next Saturday's game. While whining makes
your coach want to do anything *but* start you, getting the ball over the
plate and getting more RBIs leaves him no choice. You can even try to
act like it's a done deal by strutting onto the field and practicing like you
are already the starting pitcher. Stop thinking of yourself as second
string. In the words of great softball fans everywhere . . . we want a
pitcher, not a belly itcher. And don't forget to have fun!

e-vite rewrite

CURRENT E-VITE	E-VITE REWRITE
I am so bad at math.	*I have not done well in the past, but I am going to get the help I need to catch up. I do well in some of my other subjects. It makes sense that I can do well in math too.*
I hate my History teacher.	*I don't really know what the deal is with my history teacher, but his issues probably have nothing to do with me. I go to History to learn about Europe, not to be best friends with my teacher.*
I try out for the cheerleading squad every year and never get picked.	*Now I understand how the judging works and I can jump higher than I could last year. If I want, I could also join the pep club.*
School is really hard for me.	*I've been successful in other things before. Maybe I can get some extra help from a tutor or my teacher.*
There is not enough time in the day to do everything.	*I can adjust my schedule to fit things in that are important to me.*
Nothing they're teaching me in school will ever matter in the real world.	*Some things I learn in school will come in handy later in life. And I can't wait to get to college and choose what I want to study.*

your 'rents—the old people down the hall

Pop Quiz: Test Your Parent Energy

1. You are dying to get a car but your parents won't buy you one. You think:

   A. *This is SO UNFAIR! Everyone buys their kid a BMW these days.*

   B. *I can probably get a used car if I increase my babysitting hours. I hear the Marshalls are looking for some extra help this summer.*

   c. *I could get a ride to school with Eliza. Her parents are so much cooler than mine.*

2. Your parents drag you along to the movies and while you are there, you see a group of kids from your school laughing. You . . .

   A. *hide and pray they aren't already laughing at you.*

   B. *get up the nerve to say hi, but find yourself dissing your parents to sound cool.*

   c. *wave and go into the theater—this movie has good reviews.*

3. Your mom shows up to your field hockey game wearing the most embarrassing sweater: the one with a felt reindeer on it that lights up when she cheers. You ...

   A. *giggle to yourself about your mom's unique taste.*

   B. *lose your temper after you lose the game and tell your mom her fashion faux pas is the reason.*

   C. *secretly leave catalogs of cooler clothes on her night table, and spend hours hiding her more offensive outfits.*

4. You think you walked in on your parents kissing. You ...

   A. *joke about it with your friends but secretly wonder if you will ever be able to wipe the image out of your mind.*

   B. *think that's kind of nice.*

   C. *replay the scene over and over in your mind. You'll be nauseous and scarred for life. And, by the way, was that a little tongue I saw?*

5. Your mom and dad are insisting that you get a boring office job this summer. You think:

   A. *The money will be great, but you know in your heart you'll be miserable.*

   B. *None of your friends will be working. Why did you get stuck with parents who are so strict?*

   C. *You would much rather work as a lifeguard so you can get the perfect tan and that back-from-the-beach hair. You'll discuss this with them.*

6. Your parents always seem to let your brother do whatever he wants. It's because . . .

A. *your parents have always liked him best. It's just the way it is in your house.*

B. *your brother is really manipulative, but maybe he deserves some credit for always knowing what he wants.*

C. *he's really good at negotiating with them. Maybe you could learn a thing or two.*

7. Your mom doesn't trust you when you go out. You have the earliest curfew of anyone you know. You think:

A. *Your friends' parents are so much cooler than yours. There's no hope for you.*

B. *I'll stay out later and show them I can have fun and stay in control.*

C. *I can find ways to show my parents that I am responsible.*

8. When your dad asks you to work on your English essay, you say:

A. *"Sure," and figure out how efficiently you can do it so you can hang out with your friends later.*

B. *"In a minute." You are in the middle of your favorite TV show.*

C. *"Sure," but silently hate every minute of it. I mean, is this a sweatshop or what?*

9. Your mom is telling you to eat healthy things as she sucks down a Diet Coke for lunch. You think:

A. *What a hypocrite. She is always saying one thing and doing another.*

B. *She always has such good advice, if only she could practice what she preaches.*

c. *She means well. Now if only you could be as thin as she is.*

10. You ended up with one of those buddy moms. (Think the mom in *Mean Girls* offering snacks and condoms. Embarrassing!) She plops down on the sofa with you and your friends and wants to know all the gossip. It makes you totally uncomfortable when she asks you and your friends about who's hooking up with who. You . . .

A. *try to pretend it's no big deal. Then vent about it to your friends behind your mom's back.*

B. *scream at her in front of your friends, "You're a freak. Now leave us alone!"*

c. *explain in private, "Sorry, Mom, I don't really feel like talking to you about what my friends are doing."*

Score it: Give yourself the appropriate number of points for each answer.

1. a = 3, b = 1, c = 2	**6.** a = 3, b = 2, c = 1
2. a = 3, b = 2, c = 1	**7.** a = 3, b = 2, c = 1
3. a = 1, b =3, c = 2	**8.** a = 1, b = 2, c = 3
4. a = 2, b = 1, c = 3	**9.** a = 3, b = 1, c = 2
5. a = 2, b = 3, c = 1	**10.** a = 2, b = 3, c = 1

10-14: *You're handling your parents in a very effective way, and you are about as close to finding peace with your parents as any teenager we know. You don't take their craziness too seriously and are very clear about what you want. You will be treated as an adult by them sooner rather than later.*

15-25: *You are really just a few sarcastic comments from being in the first category. You definitely have a sense of humor about your parents but you have to try to shift your focus away from what they are that drives you crazy to what they are that you love. Sure, they're embarrassing, shortsighted, and sometimes unfair, but they are also your biggest fans.*

26-30: *You are living in a war zone and no one's coming out a winner. Too many things you are saying and doing are knee-jerk reactions and may be coming across as big jerk reactions. Try to lighten up on them a little, shift the focus of your E-vites, and they'll feel a little more relaxed too.*

This Is the Deal

Can't live with 'em, don't have anyplace to live without 'em. There is no conflict more brutal than knowing that you are practically an adult and are capable of making your own decisions, yet you are required by law and society to live under the rule of these irrational tyrants. Maybe that's a little much. But we know it sometimes feels that way. In your heart you love them, but you are certain they don't understand you. After all, how could anyone who wears her jeans up past her belly button understand you?

You don't want to hear this, but let's review a few facts about your parents. They weren't always this goofy. They were young once; they went to parties; they worried they'd never meet someone and fall in love; they stressed over their friends. And, oh yeah, they thought their parents were completely lame too. They did everything that you are doing, only most likely a lot later in life. Their real problem is that when they look at you and see you standing there with boobs and makeup and car keys in your hand, what they see is you at age three dressed up in mom's high heels and playing with your Fisher Price school bus. It's not pretty, but that's reality.

As much as it seems like it, they don't really want to eliminate all fun from your life. They just want you to be safe, and they want you to grow up to be a strong, happy, responsible person. And maybe support them when they are old. But let's not get ahead of ourselves. Here are some major beefs some girls we know have about their parents. Ring any bells?

TO: **Click!**
FROM: **Caged Animal**
RE: **Help!**

. . . .

My parents have me under house arrest! All my friends stay out until at least midnight and I'm under lock and key by eleven. I can never even get a ride home because I'm the only loser leaving the party. My parents drive up in their pajamas and honk. What is the matter with them? They treat me like a baby!

It's not that your parents believe that the Boogy Man comes out at eleven. It's just that (now here is The Truth Revealed; get out your highlighters) they hold their breath every moment that you are out. And your particular parents do not have the lung capacity to hold their breath past eleven. It's as simple as that.

You are about to click send on: *Makes sense but that blows,* right? Let's start by identifying what you want. Can we wager a guess? You want freedom. You want to be able to move through this world making decisions, learning your lessons, and enjoying every moment of it on your terms. Everybody wants that and deserves it. Isn't it even in the Bill of Rights? Let's see if we can get you a little closer to time off for good behavior.

You want more freedom, but right now you are telling them that you are not ready for it. If you are (1) stomping your feet, (2) working your voice into a full rant, and (3) shouting, "You treat me like a baby!!" then congratulations! You have just clicked send on a screaming E-vite: *My parents treat me like a baby.* And how could your RSVP be anything but yes?

Maybe by *acting like it's a done deal,* you can sneak a little responsibility into the equation. If you want them to treat you like an adult, start thinking like one. Like next time you ask to borrow the car, do it while you are unloading the dishwasher. Quiet E-vite: *I am a helpful and responsible person.* Think a few steps ahead and approach it from their perspective: "Hey, Mom, can I stay at Emily's party Saturday night until midnight? I know my curfew is eleven, but the band is starting at nine thirty p.m. and I really want to hear the whole concert. I'll call you at eleven to check in, so you know that I'm okay." The energy that you are putting out is responsible, thoughtful, and logical. You don't feel like any three-year-old we've ever met. Your parents know exactly what you are doing and why. They no longer think you want to stay out the extra hour to get pregnant in the back of a car. And you have offered them this very compassionate moment to take a breath at eleven. E-vite: *I am nearly an adult.* RSVP: *Yes.* (Don't forget to follow through with that eleven o'clock call you promised.)

TO: **Click!**
FROM: **Clone**
RE: **Help!**
. . . .

My parents have no clue who I am. This morning I walked into the kitchen and found them drooling over this catalog for a debate camp. They want me to spend the summer with a bunch of freaks learning how to argue, because it is supposed to prepare me for law school one day. My mom is literally obsessed with law school and blows me off any time I tell her I'm not into it. It was always her dream to go to law school, but she got pregnant with me in college and never went. It seems like now it's my problem and I have to live out this stupid dream just to make it up to her! Why can't she just let me be myself?

↪ **Reply:**
. . . .

This is a common problem with parents. If there was a twelve-step program for it, most parents would be required by law to attend. ("My name is Kathy, and I want my daughter to fulfill all my dreams." "Hi,

Kathy!") This isn't your problem, but you need to find a way to feel better about this so you can start E-viting in a better situation.

Parents (news flash!) are people. And as people, they have hopes and dreams. They had a quarter of a lifetime of successes and disappointments before you were born. Their emotional baggage has been neatly stowed in the overhead compartment and it's here to stay. (And don't try to mess with it, items may have shifted during flight and all that.) Like most people, they have an idea about what happiness and success look like. For your mom, happiness and success come wrapped in a law school diploma.

You want to shout, "I am NOT YOU." And when you tell them you are not interested in tennis camp or piano lessons or getting married or even being straight, you find yourself feeling really angry at them. Of course you're angry, because they seem so narrow-minded. And while it's your natural instinct to be true to who you really are (Bravo!), you also have a natural instinct to want to please your parents. So here you are, in conflict with yourself and clicking send on a bunch of crap. (Excuse me? Did Dr. Phil just enter the building??)

Search what is inside you, observe what is around you, and make a happy match. If you are an opera singer inside, please don't become a lawyer. If you dream of running the FBI, please don't become a kindergarten teacher. Your parents adore you and want you to be happy, but they just don't know what happy looks like to you. It's your job to show them what happy looks like for you. The only way to do that, of course, is by being happy. This is where turning around your E-vites comes in.

Where is your focus? *They don't understand me; they are trying to live my life; they don't even know me. I'll show them what I think of them and their stupid debate camp.* Makes sense. But try focusing on where you want to be, rather than where you are. What would it feel like if you and your parents were getting along like Mr. and Mrs. Camden in *7th Heaven.* What if you were completely free to pursue your interests with their total support? Wouldn't that feel great? E-vite: *Acceptance, love, and self-discovery.* RSVP: *Yes.*

If you can get there, click send on: *My parents love me. They know what they want. And I know what I want. I am listening to my gut about what really makes me happy. I hope they are happy with themselves, too.*

TO: **Click!**
FROM: **Open-Minded**
RE: **Help!**

· ·

My parents hate some of my best friends. They like Aisha because they play tennis with her parents and have known her forever. In fact, they like all of my friends who fit into the neat little mold of who I am supposed to hang out with. But the other night I invited my friend Terry, who's gay, and my emo friend Michael over and they totally freaked out. All of a sudden they are paranoid about where I'm going and what I'm doing. What they don't know is that these guys are really cool, and that Aisha and her friends are all stoned half the time. How can my own parents be so stupid?

↺ **Reply:**

· ·

Jump into a time machine for a minute, and let's look at your parents
again. When they were growing up, the real rebel in the community
distinguished himself by wearing hair gel. No one had the courage to
admit they were gay or even talk about the fact that straight kids were
sexually active. There was maybe one family in the neighborhood
who didn't share their religion. We're not talking cross burners here,
but there was certainly not as much open diversity back then as there
is now. It's hard for them to adjust.

Be grateful you were born when you were. Raging against your
parents about this sends this E-vite: *My parents and I are strangers.*
And chances are they'll get that vibe and think, *She's so estranged
from us. It must be that kid she's been hanging around with.* Instead,
focus on what you really like about your friends. Mention cool things
about them in a natural way around the house. When ignorance and
acceptance face off, ignorance always gets its butt kicked. Click send
on: *Acceptance and compassion.* RSVP: *Yes.*

TO: **Click**
FROM: **Under Pressure**
RE: **Help!**

· ·

*I'm fifteen years old and I am totally strung out. I'm at school from eight to three;
I play two varsity sports; I have cello lessons and newspaper staff meetings
twice a week before school. I am up until midnight doing my homework every
night and have no time to just hang with my friends. I have developed all these*

weird nervous habits like picking at my nails and pulling out my hair. I am totally

embarrassed by them, but I can't stop. My parents are wigged out over my

getting into college, but I will be completely fried by then!

↩ **Reply:**
....

The funny thing—if there is a funny thing here—is that when your parents were your age, they were hanging out pretty much full time. The crazy reality that we have created tells us that everything has to be better, faster, thinner. Like you're an iPod. Your parents think they are doing everything possible for you, but they are probably not hearing you say you're tired because you're never home.

Again, let's zero in on what you want. If you have been working this hard, you probably want to go to a good college too. You are talented and motivated, but, like peanut butter on a cracker, if you're spread too thin, you're useless. Right now you're so tired that you just want to quit everything, get in bed, and catch up on the first season of *Lost* (no, that's too complicated even—try *Real World*). But that's not really what you want either.

Outline the things you want and tell your parents how you feel. If you can't figure out what to blow off, go to two places: (1) your gut, which is constantly shouting, "Pick me! Pick me!" and (2) your college guidance counselor. He or she will help you manage your résumé to please your dream school, while cutting out a bunch of stuff that doesn't matter. We checked out a list of things the admissions committee at several colleges and universities are really looking for. "Hospitalized for Exhaustion" wasn't one of them.

Take a deep breath. You are only as stressed as you think you are. Take your focus off of being overwhelmed and focus on what you want to do. Take out your journal, look at what's on your agenda, and *write your story* about how you want your life to look. Maybe you want to really focus on your field hockey this year. And your role on the yearbook doesn't mean as much to you as playing cello in the community orchestra. Maybe your grades would be even better, with less work, if you weren't so wiped out. Maybe life is about picking the best things that you love, doing them, and feeling great. E-vite: *Success and peace in balance.* RSVP: *Yes.*

TO: **Click!**
FROM: **Clock Stopper**
RE: **Help!**

....

Things are really busy for my family right now. My dad is traveling a lot and my mom just got a new job. I feel like I have no parents anymore. All the other parents show up at school events with snacks and smiles. My parents can't even remember my best friend's name. I just want to have the mom in the minivan who has nothing on her mind but what's for dinner.

↻ **Reply:**

....

It's hard feeling like you are the only one who doesn't have something. It's worse when that something is as important as a parent. A parent returning to work can be hard on everybody in a family and it sounds like you're bearing the brunt of it. Your E-vite is focused on lack: *I am alone.*

It may be hard to get there but the first thing to do is to *get some 'tude* about how hard your parents are working to provide you with the life they think you need. It's easy to play the V-card, especially on those days when you are the last person to be picked up from school. But can you focus on how much your parents' work ethic is contributing to your character? Is there something cool about your parents' jobs that you can learn from?

Don't start feeling disconnected because your parents are not there all the time. Connect with them when they are around. When they are not, turn to your best friends, your teachers, your coaches, and other family members. Get involved with sports and clubs, and feel good about your life. Remember that you are never alone and are an important part of this world. E-vite: *I am connected.* RSVP: *Yes.* You may even find that the time together with your parents is more rewarding now than it was when they were always there.

e-vite rewrite

CURRENT E-VITE	E-VITE REWRITE
My parents are too strict.	*My parents have been flexible in the past. I bet there is a way to build trust.*
My parents are totally overprotective.	*They really care about what happens to me. Right now, I don't have to worry about making a lot of choices that I don't feel ready to make.*
My parents don't let me do anything.	*They do let me do some things. There must be a way to make them see how responsible I am.*

My parents don't listen to me.	*I think it's possible that I can be heard and understood. We used to communicate so well when I was younger. I think we can do it again.*
My parents are totally out of touch with my generation.	*My generation is really different from my parents', but they do try to understand some of my issues.*

doom and gloom

Pop Quiz: Test Your Energy About Our World

1. The weather report says today's temperature reached a high of one hundred degrees. It broke the record set in 1912. You think:

   A. *Global warming is ruining our planet. We're all going to be fried in twenty years.*

   B. *Some days are just plain hot. If it was this hot in 1912, perhaps this isn't a result of global warming.*

   c. *What's the big deal? Thanks to my AC, I never even knew how hot it got.*

2. You read in the newspaper that some brands of pet food have been recalled due to contamination. You think:

A. *If they can't control dog food, then they certainly can't control people food. It will be no time at all before people are dying, not just animals.*

B. *I could text my friends who have pets, but why bother? All this stuff is just hype to scare people into watching the news.*

c. *I haven't heard of any other problems, but if they come up, we'll figure out how to deal with them.*

3. On Earth Day you . . .

   A. *celebrate the wondrous, beautiful planet we all live on.*

   B. *notice how much more polluted the air seems now than when you were a kid.*

   c. *fight for the health of our planet by passing out brochures about pollution.*

4. You just paid a fortune to fill up the car with gas. You think:

   A. *These prices are insane. Now I can barely afford to go to the movies.*

   B. *Hey . . . wouldn't it be cool to start carpooling to school with a friend? I could start saving for that Ella Moss dress I've had my eye on.*

   c. *It's cool how Leonardo DiCaprio drives a Prius. I feel bad that our SUV guzzles so much gas.*

5. A new report by the EPA says pollution is down compared to last year. You think:

   A. *Obviously this is just more propaganda from the government. It's useless. Our government can't be trusted.*

   B. *Hey, that's pretty cool.*

   C. *That's amazing news! But I feel exhausted just thinking about how long it will take to fix the hole in the ozone layer.*

6. It's hurricane season again and your town has been affected previously. You think:

   A. *I'm a little frightened, but I bet there are ways my parents can fix our house so it can withstand weather like this.*

   B. *OMG, maybe we should just move. I am so freaked out by the idea of moving. I don't want to have to switch schools.*

   C. *I think my house is safe, but I am sick and tired of hearing about everyone else's drama.*

7. When you watch the news about a tragic event in another country, you think:

   A. *It's so unfair that people in other countries have to live in such horrible conditions. I feel guilty about how comparatively easy my life is.*

   B. *Maybe our country will give humanitarian aid. It makes me feel good to know that some of our tax dollars will go to help.*

c. *Maybe things will get better for them soon. I am terrified something like that will happen here.*

8. A tsunami just hit and thousands of people died. You think:

A. *I am so appreciative of my life and I plan on contributing to the relief fund.*

B. *I want to cry.*

c. *I understand that death is part of life. It just makes me so upset to think of so many people dying at one time.*

9. When Angelina Jolie adopted yet another baby, you thought:

A. *It feels good to see that baby find a safe place to live.*

B. *What a noble cause, but enough is enough!*

c. *Poor Brad.*

10. You hear news that the dolphin population is finally increasing. You think:

A. *Thank goodness. Now I can eat tuna again.*

B. *I like to envision a government that keeps looking after our environment.*

c. *What about all the other ecosystems we've destroyed? It's a lost cause.*

Score it: Give yourself the appropriate number of points for each answer.

1. a = 3, b = 1, c = 2   **6.** a = 1, b = 3, c = 2
2. a = 3, b = 2, c = 1   **7.** a = 3, b = 1, c = 2
3. a = 1, b = 3, c = 2   **8.** a = 1, b = 3, c = 2
4. a = 3, b = 1, c = 2   **9.** a = 1, b = 2, c = 3
5. a = 3, b = 1, c = 2   **10.** a = 2, b = 1, c = 3

10-14: *Little Miss Sunshine, you are there! You look on the bright side; you focus on the aspect of every situation that feels good. Your energy is designing the world that you want to live in. On behalf of the other 6,602,224,174 (and counting) people in the world, we thank you.*

15-25: *You're so close we can taste it. Your energy is mostly positive but you aren't going all the way with it. You have a great thought, then you quickly bring something to mind that messes up your E-vite. You're happy but . . . It's all good and yet . . . Just try to stop yourself before you go there.*

26–30: *The media loves you, baby. You are the kind of person who keeps the media on the hunt for injustices to exaggerate and pain to exploit. Please read on, we beg you. We just have to dig out the glimmer of hope that's buried under that Panic Poncho that's weighing you down. Start feeling a little better about something and you'll end up feeling a lot better about everything.*

This Is the Deal

If you happened to pick up a paper this morning, you probably saw the news: THE SKY IS FALLING! We're not sure if they've gotten their facts straight, but it seems like that's the message we are reading every day. To hear it told, we should be having 800 degree Novembers by 2050 and there's one barrel of oil left for all of us to share.

But, okay, we'll admit, things do need to change. Global warming is real; we use up too much of everything and recycle too little. Our natural resources have been compromised by our efforts at progress. Something has to give. And it is! What's "giving" is a new generation of green-minded people: a generation of people who are truly focused on solving this problem. (In case you're not following, we mean you guys.)

You are the generation who got it right away. You understand why Cameron Diaz did MTV's green-minded *Trippin*. It doesn't surprise you that Leo has dedicated himself as much to our planet as to his career. It doesn't make him some kind of freak to speak out about the environment. In fact (if this is at all possible), it made him hotter.

And the most important thing that you can do to help is send out the right E-vites. When you see the news about the polar ice caps and the endangered rain forest, don't click send on: *The end is near!* Focus on what you can be doing and do something. The generations before you have already taken on the role of being part of the problem; you guys know how to be part of the solution.

Every time I pick up a paper or turn on the TV, it's violence everywhere. I don't just mean the horrible wars, I mean on the streets close to me. I feel totally helpless; I have no control.

↩ **Reply:**

We hear you. The violence in the world is horrible. But we are not going to help it by clicking send on: *I am helpless!* This is a great time to turn your focus onto what you want, and to take steps to make it happen. We imagine you want to feel safe in your community and to know that people around the world are enjoying the same level of security.

We recommend that you *visualize your course,* which is really everyone's course. Can you channel John Lennon and just imagine? Picture more peaceful neighborhoods around you and project that peace across the world. This was done successfully in Washington, DC, in the early 1990s, when a group of people led by John Hagelin, PhD, gathered for meditation to bring about peace in their community. Violent crimes in that city decreased by 23 percent!

Once you've done that, *get some action.* What can you do to feel less panicked? Monitor how much violence you are watching on TV, online, on You Tube, and at the movies. Find websites where you can stay up to date on current events without having to look at violent photographs. Do anything you can to find a way to click send on: *Peace.*

My neighbor just got diagnosed with a melanoma. She had it removed but it could have been really serious. When my mom was a kid, no one ever talked about skin cancer. They did all the same stuff we do, but we're the ones getting screwed because of the ozone problem.

↩ **Reply:**

It's true that the problem was not as bad when your parents were kids. But just remember that with problems come solutions. Think of it this way: With the hole in the ozone came the invention of waterproof SPF 50. Today we have the problem, but also the knowledge and the technology to protect ourselves. Your fear of skin cancer is making you send out this E-vite: *I have no control, I am a victim of the environment.* That's not doing you any good at all.

When you heard about your neighbor's horrible diagnosis, you probably had a strong feeling of how important it is to you to be healthy. Click send on that: *I want to be healthy.* Don't get yourself into a rut, ruminating over every freckle on your body, searching the Internet for photos of a mole just exactly like yours. Be smart, get yourself checked, then put on your sunscreen, and get back to the business of having a great life.

* *

I did my science project on solar panels and how we can use them to power our homes in the future. The good news is that I won the Science Fair and my teachers were really impressed by all the research I did. The annoying news is that they just sort of dismissed it as an idea that wasn't really going to catch on. I told them how lots of homes were being built with solar panels now, but one teacher said that the idea would never catch on because the big corporations can't profit from the sun. Is money all anyone cares about? Are we going to destroy the planet to make a buck? I feel like our priorities are all screwed up.

↩ **Reply:**

* *

We hear you, and this is a legitimate problem. In industry, decisions are made to maximize the value of the companies involved, and often the greater good is overlooked. It feels overwhelming to try to compete with the goals of a multibillion dollar corporation. It makes you want to shrug and say, "Why bother?" The E-vite you are sending is this: *I am fearful and powerless.* And we don't blame you at all.

There is another way to look at this, though. Never before have voters been more green-minded. These environmentally conscious people are voting to elect the next wave of representatives and senators, who will likely pass reforms to make corporations tune in to the bigger picture. As voters and shoppers, individuals make choices all the time about which companies to support and which politicians to elect. We recommend you *get some action.* Stay involved with the idea of solar panels, and talk about it whenever you can. The more people who are interested in them, and who eventually adapt their lifestyles to include them, the better. Plus, there are lots of mechanisms for sharing your ideas. Is there an environmental club you can join at school? If not, consider starting one. Join an online community dedicated to improving the environment and research solar panels. Write to your congressperson. You will be sending out a new E-vite: *It is possible to change the world.*

TO: **Click!**
FROM: **Getting Warmer**
RE: **Help**

. . . .

I saw An Inconvenient Truth *this weekend and I am so freaked out about global warming. I totally get how horrible what we are doing is to the environment. But my parents just got this huge SUV that guzzles gas and, well, I really love it. I have so many different things plugged into the wall in my room, and they all use up a ton of electricity. When I go to the cafeteria at lunch, I can't get over how much garbage there is. I feel so guilty all the time for wanting to live the way I do. As much as I want to help, I don't want to go live on a mountain somewhere and start using leaves for toilet paper!*

↩ **Reply:**

. . . .

We've all gotten really used to all of our energy-sucking gadgets. Let's face it, they make our lives easier and more fun. We don't want to skateboard down the freeway to get to New York City either. Although it's easy to feel guilty about our country's crazy consumption habit, feeling guilty doesn't help solve the problem. The only E-vite guilt sends out is this: *I feel awful and I am part of the problem.* RSVP: Yes.

What we think you are really wanting is to be part of the solution without giving up all of the convenience of your lifestyle. We applaud you for this not only on behalf of the earth, but on behalf of yourself too. But if your gas-guzzlin' family vacation has become more of a guilt trip than a road trip, your backseat angst is just sending out more negative E-vites and not helping anyone. Instead, get in sync with what you want: to live a greener life.

We'd like you to *get some action* but please don't start shopping for a new tent just yet. Let's start a little smaller. Is it really that inconvenient to choose paper over plastic at the supermarket? Is it really that much harder to bring your own canvas bags? Pick out some chic ones and own the look of Green Girl. Is it really so hard to turn off the power to both the TV *and* the cable box when you're done watching? Is it such a big deal to unplug your hairdryer? Of course not, and if you can do these tiny things then you are now part of the solution. And why not check out www.liveearth.org for additional ideas? You'll keep clicking send on: *I feel great about what I'm doing.* And more energy-saving ideas will be part of your RSVP.

TO: **Click!**
FROM: **Terrorized**
RE: **Help!**
. . . .

I am terrified of terrorists. My best friend's dad was killed in the Twin Towers on September 11. He almost got out right before the North Tower collapsed. I am haunted by everything that happened that day and feel like my world will never be the same. There are so many places I want to go see, but every time I think of getting on an airplane I envision the worst. Ever since September 11, I really do

feel like there is a "monster in my closet," like someone's out to get me.

↩ **Reply:**

. . . .

And that's why they call them "terrorists," rather than "happy sunshine guys." The amazing thing that terrorists have been able to do from thousands of miles away is rob us of our sense of security and, in extreme cases, take away the joy we used to feel in normal everyday things. You almost applaud them, as this isn't easy to do. But let's NOT applaud them and let's stop them where we can. Let's send a better E-vite than: *I am terrified.*

There is a different way to look at this. There have been wars and terror and atrocities forever, even before CNN started packaging it and pumping it into our homes like raw sewage. This is not a new thing; the new thing is that the stench has gotten too bad to ignore. And while it's evident that there are people, governments, and nations working to destroy us, there are more people, governments, and nations working 24/7 to protect us.

Like the environment, we all need to be healed. Rather than being paralyzed with fear (Results are in: They win!), try to focus on what you can control and what you want. Focus on your own sense of well-being and safety. Imagine a world that looks the way you wish it did. Focus on religious tolerance, focus on acceptance. Your E-vite reads: *Peace.* RSVP: *Yes.*

e-vite rewrite

CURRENT E-VITE	E-VITE REWRITE
They are coming to get us!	*There are thousands of people who devote their lives to keeping me safe.*
We are ruining the earth.	*There are so many things that I can do to conserve and protect the environment.*
People all over the world are killing each other.	*The world has always known violence and has recovered from it.*
There are just too many fundamental differences between cultures around the world for us ever to be at peace.	*It's easier to travel now than ever. Maybe exposure to new cultures through travel will promote tolerance.*
I'm afraid to grow up and bring children into this world.	*If I decide to have children, I will teach them everything I can about peace.*
The weather seems so unpredictable lately.	*The environment is constantly changing. I can do things to keep myself safe.*

daily journal
(get clickin')

WE KNOW HOW BUSY YOU ARE. Never in history have teenagers been so busy. Even the pioneers got to call it quits when the sun went down. You? There's school, sports, activities, part-time jobs, homework, and constantly ringing and vibrating cell phones. Ideally, we would want you to spend fifteen minutes a day on this journal. Many (okay, most) days you'll have five. That's fine. If you fill out even one or two of these boxes it will dramatically change your energy regarding the thing that you want. Fill them all out, and you'll just get your RSVP faster. But don't be hard on yourself if you miss a day or if you only have time to write "Want new boyfriend." Anything is better than nothing, and the effect is cumulative. If you start feeling a little more enthusiastic about what you want, it will be easier to keep feeling good and clicking send on more positive E-vites. We have included at the beginning of the journal an entry from a sample day, just to get you started.

All right, gals, sharpen your pencils and get ready to have fun redesigning your life. The next four weeks are completely up to you, so have fun and enjoy clicking away! As Natasha Bedingfield would say, today is where your book begins . . . The rest is still unwritten.

like you needed
one more thing to do

BY NOW, YOU PROBABLY GET IT. But the best way to make this work for you is to get to work yourself. What follows is a daily journal that will take you through four weeks of writing better E-vites. It takes approximately twenty-eight days to form a new habit. We think that the amount of time it will take you to shift your focus and get in sync with what you want will depend on where you are today. For some of you it'll be faster, for others it will take longer. For all of you, it will be a huge challenge. Embrace it.

On the left side of each journal page is your space for making it happen. Write down what you want, write about how it's going to be. Paste a picture or draw something that represents what you want. Really get into the details so that you can feel yourself getting excited about it. If you can feel it, you've clicked send.

On the right side of the page is a day planner. This is where you meet the Universe halfway. What are you going to do to make room in your life for all the great new stuff coming your way? Keep track of your assignments, sports practices, extracurriculars, dates . . . whatever you've got on your plate. Seeing it all laid out in front of you will help you *get grounded* and stay focused.

Most important, be creative in this process. Take our ideas and add your own. Get in sync in a way that feels fun for you and you'll be clicking send on the best E-vites yet.

sample day

IM Phrase: It's going to be great when . . .

I get a summer job lifeguarding at Santa Monica beach.

This is how it's going to be . . .

It will be a dream come true to get paid (well!) for hanging out on the beach, getting tan, and staying in shape all summer. I will be working with the cutest guys in the world every day—even Jack Sims will be working at the beach. On our lunch breaks we will walk down to the pier, talk about what parties are on for that night. I'll always know exactly what is going on because I'll spend my day where all the best plans are started. At the end of the summer I will be in amazing shape for swim team. The college recruiters are going to start coming to our meets and they are definitely going to notice me. I will cut seconds off of my freestyle time after having swum in the ocean for two months. Life is good!

I want this because it will make me feel . . .

1. independent

2. happy

3. in the loop!

That's where I'll focus!

Plan B . . .

It might also be cool to have a job as a salesperson at the Gap!

I am grateful for:

1. my health

2. my strength as a swimmer

3. that I live near the beach!

Thoughts to click send on:

I have always been a very strong swimmer.

The kids who got the jobs last summer were my age and had my swim team experience.

Last summer I got the job I wanted, why not again?

7:00		**To-Do List for My Goal:**
		Pick up school application
7:30		*Find CPR certificate*
8:00		
8:30		
9:00		
9:30		
10:00		**To-Do List for Plan B:**
		Talk to Amy about her experience
10:30		*last summer*
11:00		*Check out Gap online*
11:30		
12:00	*Amy*	
12:30		
1:00		**Assignments:**
		history proj.
1:30		*English test Wed.*
2:00		
2:30		
3:00	*yearbook layout*	
3:30		
4:00		**Tomorrow will look like this:**
4:30		*Tomorrow, I will wake up full of*
		energy for swim practice. The line
5:00	*meet Ally about com. service*	*will be short at Starbucks. I will*
5:30		*show my coach that I am ready*
		to lead our team in freestyle. I
6:00		*will finish my history project early*
6:30		*and easily. When I see Jack Sims,*
7:00		*I will be calm and say something*
		cool.
7:30		
8:00		

IM Phrase: It's going to be great when . . .

This is how it's going to be . . .

I want this because it will make me feel . . .

Plan B . . .

I am grateful for:

Thoughts to click send on:

That's where I'll focus!

Time		Section
7:00		To-Do List for my Goal:
7:30		
8:00		
8:30		
9:00		
9:30		
10:00		To-Do List for Plan B:
10:30		
11:00		
11:30		
12:00		
12:30		
1:00		Assignments:
1:30		
2:00		
2:30		
3:00		
3:30		
4:00		Tomorrow will look like this:
4:30		
5:00		
5:30		
6:00		
6:30		
7:00		
7:30		
8:00		

IM Phrase: It's going to be great when . . .

This is how it's going to be . . .

I want this because
it will make me feel . . .

Plan B . . .

I am grateful for:

Thoughts to click send on:

That's where I'll focus!

Time	
7:00	**To-Do List for my Goal:**
7:30	
8:00	
8:30	
9:00	
9:30	
10:00	**To-Do List for Plan B:**
10:30	
11:00	
11:30	
12:00	
12:30	
1:00	**Assignments:**
1:30	
2:00	
2:30	
3:00	
3:30	
4:00	**Tomorrow will look like this:**
4:30	
5:00	
5:30	
6:00	
6:30	
7:00	
7:30	
8:00	

IM Phrase: It's going to be great when . . .

This is how it's going to be . . .

I want this because
it will make me feel . . .

Plan B . . .

I am grateful for:

Thoughts to click send on:

That's where I'll focus!

Time	
7:00	To-Do List for my Goal:
7:30	
8:00	
8:30	
9:00	
9:30	
10:00	To-Do List for Plan B:
10:30	
11:00	
11:30	
12:00	
12:30	
1:00	Assignments:
1:30	
2:00	
2:30	
3:00	
3:30	
4:00	Tomorrow will look like this:
4:30	
5:00	
5:30	
6:00	
6:30	
7:00	
7:30	
8:00	

IM Phrase: It's going to be great when . . .

This is how it's going to be . . .

I want this because
it will make me feel . . .

Plan B . . .

I am grateful for:

Thoughts to click send on:

That's where I'll focus!

Time	
7:00	To-Do List for my Goal:
7:30	
8:00	
8:30	
9:00	
9:30	
10:00	To-Do List for Plan B:
10:30	
11:00	
11:30	
12:00	
12:30	
1:00	Assignments:
1:30	
2:00	
2:30	
3:00	
3:30	
4:00	Tomorrow will look like this:
4:30	
5:00	
5:30	
6:00	
6:30	
7:00	
7:30	
8:00	

IM Phrase: It's going to be great when . . .

This is how it's going to be . . .

I want this because
it will make me feel . . .

Plan B . . .

I am grateful for:

Thoughts to click send on:

That's where I'll focus!

Time	
7:00	To-Do List for my Goal:
7:30	
8:00	
8:30	
9:00	
9:30	
10:00	To-Do List for Plan B:
10:30	
11:00	
11:30	
12:00	
12:30	
1:00	Assignments:
1:30	
2:00	
2:30	
3:00	
3:30	
4:00	Tomorrow will look like this:
4:30	
5:00	
5:30	
6:00	
6:30	
7:00	
7:30	
8:00	

IM Phrase: It's going to be great when . . .

This is how it's going to be . . .

I want this because
it will make me feel . . .

Plan B . . .

I am grateful for:

Thoughts to click send on:

That's where I'll focus!

Time	
7:00	To-Do List for my Goal:
7:30	
8:00	
8:30	
9:00	
9:30	
10:00	To-Do List for Plan B:
10:30	
11:00	
11:30	
12:00	
12:30	
1:00	Assignments:
1:30	
2:00	
2:30	
3:00	
3:30	
4:00	Tomorrow will look like this:
4:30	
5:00	
5:30	
6:00	
6:30	
7:00	
7:30	
8:00	

IM Phrase: It's going to be great when . . .

This is how it's going to be . . .

I want this because
it will make me feel . . .

Plan B . . .

I am grateful for:

Thoughts to click send on:

That's where I'll focus!

Time	
7:00	**To-Do List for my Goal:**
7:30	
8:00	
8:30	
9:00	
9:30	
10:00	**To-Do List for Plan B:**
10:30	
11:00	
11:30	
12:00	
12:30	
1:00	**Assignments:**
1:30	
2:00	
2:30	
3:00	
3:30	
4:00	**Tomorrow will look like this:**
4:30	
5:00	
5:30	
6:00	
6:30	
7:00	
7:30	
8:00	

IM Phrase: It's going to be great when . . .

This is how it's going to be . . .

I want this because
it will make me feel . . .

Plan B . . .

I am grateful for:

Thoughts to click send on:

That's where I'll focus!

Time	
7:00	To-Do List for my Goal:
7:30	
8:00	
8:30	
9:00	
9:30	
10:00	To-Do List for Plan B:
10:30	
11:00	
11:30	
12:00	
12:30	
1:00	Assignments:
1:30	
2:00	
2:30	
3:00	
3:30	
4:00	Tomorrow will look like this:
4:30	
5:00	
5:30	
6:00	
6:30	
7:00	
7:30	
8:00	

IM Phrase: It's going to be great when . . .

This is how it's going to be . . .

I want this because
it will make me feel . . .

Plan B . . .

I am grateful for:

Thoughts to click send on:

That's where I'll focus!

Time	
7:00	To-Do List for my Goal:
7:30	
8:00	
8:30	
9:00	
9:30	
10:00	To-Do List for Plan B:
10:30	
11:00	
11:30	
12:00	
12:30	
1:00	Assignments:
1:30	
2:00	
2:30	
3:00	
3:30	
4:00	Tomorrow will look like this:
4:30	
5:00	
5:30	
6:00	
6:30	
7:00	
7:30	
8:00	

IM Phrase: It's going to be great when . . .

This is how it's going to be . . .

I want this because
it will make me feel . . .

Plan B . . .

I am grateful for:

Thoughts to click send on:

That's where I'll focus!

7:00	To-Do List for my Goal:
7:30	
8:00	
8:30	
9:00	
9:30	
10:00	To-Do List for Plan B:
10:30	
11:00	
11:30	
12:00	
12:30	
1:00	Assignments:
1:30	
2:00	
2:30	
3:00	
3:30	
4:00	Tomorrow will look like this:
4:30	
5:00	
5:30	
6:00	
6:30	
7:00	
7:30	
8:00	

IM Phrase: It's going to be great when . . .

This is how it's going to be . . .

I want this because
it will make me feel . . .

Plan B . . .

I am grateful for:

Thoughts to click send on:

That's where I'll focus!

7:00	To-Do List for my Goal:
7:30	
8:00	
8:30	
9:00	
9:30	
10:00	To-Do List for Plan B:
10:30	
11:00	
11:30	
12:00	
12:30	
1:00	Assignments:
1:30	
2:00	
2:30	
3:00	
3:30	
4:00	Tomorrow will look like this:
4:30	
5:00	
5:30	
6:00	
6:30	
7:00	
7:30	
8:00	

IM Phrase: It's going to be great when . . .

This is how it's going to be . . .

I want this because
it will make me feel . . .

Plan B . . .

I am grateful for:

Thoughts to click send on:

That's where I'll focus!

7:00	To-Do List for my Goal:
7:30	
8:00	
8:30	
9:00	
9:30	
10:00	To-Do List for Plan B:
10:30	
11:00	
11:30	
12:00	
12:30	
1:00	Assignments:
1:30	
2:00	
2:30	
3:00	
3:30	
4:00	Tomorrow will look like this:
4:30	
5:00	
5:30	
6:00	
6:30	
7:00	
7:30	
8:00	

IM Phrase: It's going to be great when . . .

This is how it's going to be . . .

I want this because
it will make me feel . . .

Plan B . . .

I am grateful for:

Thoughts to click send on:

That's where I'll focus!

Time	
7:00	
7:30	
8:00	
8:30	
9:00	
9:30	
10:00	
10:30	
11:00	
11:30	
12:00	
12:30	
1:00	
1:30	
2:00	
2:30	
3:00	
3:30	
4:00	
4:30	
5:00	
5:30	
6:00	
6:30	
7:00	
7:30	
8:00	

To-Do List for my Goal:

To-Do List for Plan B:

Assignments:

Tomorrow will look like this:

IM Phrase: It's going to be great when . . .

This is how it's going to be . . .

I want this because it will make me feel . . .

Plan B . . .

I am grateful for:

Thoughts to click send on:

That's where I'll focus!

Time		
7:00		To-Do List for my Goal:
7:30		
8:00		
8:30		
9:00		
9:30		
10:00		To-Do List for Plan B:
10:30		
11:00		
11:30		
12:00		
12:30		
1:00		Assignments:
1:30		
2:00		
2:30		
3:00		
3:30		
4:00		Tomorrow will look like this:
4:30		
5:00		
5:30		
6:00		
6:30		
7:00		
7:30		
8:00		

IM Phrase: It's going to be great when . . .

This is how it's going to be . . .

I want this because it will make me feel . . .

Plan B . . .

I am grateful for:

Thoughts to click send on:

That's where I'll focus!

Time	
7:00	**To-Do List for my Goal:**
7:30	
8:00	
8:30	
9:00	
9:30	
10:00	**To-Do List for Plan B:**
10:30	
11:00	
11:30	
12:00	
12:30	
1:00	**Assignments:**
1:30	
2:00	
2:30	
3:00	
3:30	
4:00	**Tomorrow will look like this:**
4:30	
5:00	
5:30	
6:00	
6:30	
7:00	
7:30	
8:00	

IM Phrase: It's going to be great when . . .

This is how it's going to be . . .

I want this because
it will make me feel . . .

Plan B . . .

I am grateful for:

Thoughts to click send on:

That's where I'll focus!

Time	
7:00	
7:30	
8:00	
8:30	
9:00	
9:30	
10:00	
10:30	
11:00	
11:30	
12:00	
12:30	
1:00	
1:30	
2:00	
2:30	
3:00	
3:30	
4:00	
4:30	
5:00	
5:30	
6:00	
6:30	
7:00	
7:30	
8:00	

To-Do List for my Goal:

To-Do List for Plan B:

Assignments:

Tomorrow will look like this:

IM Phrase: It's going to be great when . . .

This is how it's going to be . . .

I want this because
it will make me feel . . .

Plan B . . .

I am grateful for:

Thoughts to click send on:

That's where I'll focus!

Time		
7:00		**To-Do List for my Goal:**
7:30		
8:00		
8:30		
9:00		
9:30		
10:00		**To-Do List for Plan B:**
10:30		
11:00		
11:30		
12:00		
12:30		
1:00		**Assignments:**
1:30		
2:00		
2:30		
3:00		
3:30		
4:00		**Tomorrow will look like this:**
4:30		
5:00		
5:30		
6:00		
6:30		
7:00		
7:30		
8:00		

IM Phrase: It's going to be great when . . .

This is how it's going to be . . .

I want this because
it will make me feel . . .

Plan B . . .

I am grateful for:

Thoughts to click send on:

That's where I'll focus!

Time	
7:00	To-Do List for my Goal:
7:30	
8:00	
8:30	
9:00	
9:30	
10:00	To-Do List for Plan B:
10:30	
11:00	
11:30	
12:00	
12:30	
1:00	Assignments:
1:30	
2:00	
2:30	
3:00	
3:30	
4:00	Tomorrow will look like this:
4:30	
5:00	
5:30	
6:00	
6:30	
7:00	
7:30	
8:00	

IM Phrase: It's going to be great when . . .

This is how it's going to be . . .

I want this because it will make me feel . . .

Plan B . . .

I am grateful for:

Thoughts to click send on:

That's where I'll focus!

Time	
7:00	To-Do List for my Goal:
7:30	
8:00	
8:30	
9:00	
9:30	
10:00	To-Do List for Plan B:
10:30	
11:00	
11:30	
12:00	
12:30	
1:00	Assignments:
1:30	
2:00	
2:30	
3:00	
3:30	
4:00	Tomorrow will look like this:
4:30	
5:00	
5:30	
6:00	
6:30	
7:00	
7:30	
8:00	

IM Phrase: It's going to be great when . . .

This is how it's going to be . . .

I want this because
it will make me feel . . .

Plan B . . .

I am grateful for:

Thoughts to click send on:

That's where I'll focus!

Time	
7:00	To-Do List for my Goal:
7:30	
8:00	
8:30	
9:00	
9:30	
10:00	To-Do List for Plan B:
10:30	
11:00	
11:30	
12:00	
12:30	
1:00	Assignments:
1:30	
2:00	
2:30	
3:00	
3:30	
4:00	Tomorrow will look like this:
4:30	
5:00	
5:30	
6:00	
6:30	
7:00	
7:30	
8:00	

IM Phrase: It's going to be great when . . .

This is how it's going to be . . .

I want this because
it will make me feel . . .

Plan B . . .

I am grateful for:

Thoughts to click send on:

That's where I'll focus!

7:00	To-Do List for my Goal:
7:30	
8:00	
8:30	
9:00	
9:30	
10:00	To-Do List for Plan B:
10:30	
11:00	
11:30	
12:00	
12:30	
1:00	Assignments:
1:30	
2:00	
2:30	
3:00	
3:30	
4:00	Tomorrow will look like this:
4:30	
5:00	
5:30	
6:00	
6:30	
7:00	
7:30	
8:00	

IM Phrase: It's going to be great when . . .

This is how it's going to be . . .

I want this because
it will make me feel . . .

Plan B . . .

I am grateful for:

Thoughts to click send on:

That's where I'll focus!

Time	
7:00	
7:30	
8:00	
8:30	
9:00	
9:30	
10:00	
10:30	
11:00	
11:30	
12:00	
12:30	
1:00	
1:30	
2:00	
2:30	
3:00	
3:30	
4:00	
4:30	
5:00	
5:30	
6:00	
6:30	
7:00	
7:30	
8:00	

To-Do List for my Goal:

To-Do List for Plan B:

Assignments:

Tomorrow will look like this:

IM Phrase: It's going to be great when . . .

This is how it's going to be . . .

I want this because it will make me feel . . .

Plan B . . .

I am grateful for:

Thoughts to click send on:

That's where I'll focus!

Time		To-Do List for my Goal:
7:00		
7:30		
8:00		
8:30		
9:00		
9:30		
10:00		To-Do List for Plan B:
10:30		
11:00		
11:30		
12:00		
12:30		
1:00		Assignments:
1:30		
2:00		
2:30		
3:00		
3:30		
4:00		Tomorrow will look like this:
4:30		
5:00		
5:30		
6:00		
6:30		
7:00		
7:30		
8:00		

IM Phrase: It's going to be great when . . .

This is how it's going to be . . .

I want this because
it will make me feel . . .

Plan B . . .

I am grateful for:

Thoughts to click send on:

That's where I'll focus!

Time	
7:00	To-Do List for my Goal:
7:30	
8:00	
8:30	
9:00	
9:30	
10:00	To-Do List for Plan B:
10:30	
11:00	
11:30	
12:00	
12:30	
1:00	Assignments:
1:30	
2:00	
2:30	
3:00	
3:30	
4:00	Tomorrow will look like this:
4:30	
5:00	
5:30	
6:00	
6:30	
7:00	
7:30	
8:00	

IM Phrase: It's going to be great when . . .

This is how it's going to be . . .

I want this because it will make me feel . . .

Plan B . . .

I am grateful for:

Thoughts to click send on:

That's where I'll focus!

	To-Do List for my Goal:
7:00	
7:30	
8:00	
8:30	
9:00	
9:30	
10:00	To-Do List for Plan B:
10:30	
11:00	
11:30	
12:00	
12:30	
1:00	Assignments:
1:30	
2:00	
2:30	
3:00	
3:30	
4:00	Tomorrow will look like this:
4:30	
5:00	
5:30	
6:00	
6:30	
7:00	
7:30	
8:00	

IM Phrase: It's going to be great when . . .

This is how it's going to be . . .

I want this because
it will make me feel . . .

Plan B . . .

I am grateful for:

Thoughts to click send on:

That's where I'll focus!

7:00	To-Do List for my Goal:
7:30	
8:00	
8:30	
9:00	
9:30	
10:00	To-Do List for Plan B:
10:30	
11:00	
11:30	
12:00	
12:30	
1:00	Assignments:
1:30	
2:00	
2:30	
3:00	
3:30	
4:00	Tomorrow will look like this:
4:30	
5:00	
5:30	
6:00	
6:30	
7:00	
7:30	
8:00	

IM Phrase: It's going to be great when . . .

This is how it's going to be . . .

I want this because
it will make me feel . . .

Plan B . . .

I am grateful for:

Thoughts to click send on:

That's where I'll focus!

Time	
7:00	To-Do List for my Goal:
7:30	
8:00	
8:30	
9:00	
9:30	
10:00	To-Do List for Plan B:
10:30	
11:00	
11:30	
12:00	
12:30	
1:00	Assignments:
1:30	
2:00	
2:30	
3:00	
3:30	
4:00	Tomorrow will look like this:
4:30	
5:00	
5:30	
6:00	
6:30	
7:00	
7:30	
8:00	

IM Phrase: It's going to be great when . . .

This is how it's going to be . . .

I want this because
it will make me feel . . .

Plan B . . .

I am grateful for:

Thoughts to click send on:

That's where I'll focus!

Time	
7:00	**To-Do List for my Goal:**
7:30	
8:00	
8:30	
9:00	
9:30	
10:00	**To-Do List for Plan B:**
10:30	
11:00	
11:30	
12:00	
12:30	
1:00	**Assignments:**
1:30	
2:00	
2:30	
3:00	
3:30	
4:00	**Tomorrow will look like this:**
4:30	
5:00	
5:30	
6:00	
6:30	
7:00	
7:30	
8:00	

Get the Lingo: A Glossary of Click! Terms

....

Army of Complainers (n.): individuals who dedicate a great deal of energy to finding something to complain about, as in, "My morning is ruined because my Frappuccino's not cold and someone just bought the last cinnamon raisin bagel."

authenticity (n.): characteristic of being true to yourself; leads to the condition of being cool

Bitching and Moaning (n.): two evil stepsisters who show up everywhere you are these days; the first enlistees in the Army of Complainers

blame game (n.): popular activity in both Blamingham and Victimville, involving attributing all your problems to other people; unlike other games, there are no winners.

Blamingham (n.): Where the blame game is played most frequently—the next town over from Victimville; as in, "She packed her bags and went to Blamingham."

boomerang (n.): curved device that, like energy, goes around and comes around

click send on something (v.): to attach great enthusiasm to it, good or bad, and invite it into your life; as in, *"The SATs are this weekend. I'll click send on feeling relaxed and clear-headed."*

desperado (n.): state of desperate neediness; often leads to poor decision-making and heightened misery; as in, "After being rejected by her crush, Dierdre got all desperado and prank called him, forgetting to block her caller ID."

energy (n.): vibration that emanates from all matter

E-vite (n.): for the purposes of this book, the energy you are sending out to the Universe to bring stuff into your life

E-vite rewrite (n.): desire that has been rephrased to make it more likely to bring you what you want

Focus Factor (n.): phenomenon of bringing into your life what you focus on, good or bad

gossip (v.): hands down the quickest way to let others know you can't be trusted (see also *boomerang*)

IM phrase (n.): positive thought about your goal that you remember to think every time you get an IM

law of E-vitation (n.): Your energy is sending out a constant stream of E-vites to the universe. The RSVP is always *Yes.*

luck (n.): the result of hard work and a great attitude

meet the Universe halfway (v.): get off the couch and take inspired action; make good stuff happen; as in, "I met the Universe halfway by striking up a conversation with my crush."

not syncin' (v.): feeling uncomfortable; getting signals that it's time to update your playlist and/or rewrite your E-vites; as in, "I'm not syncin' with my friends lately. I'd like to hang out with people with whom I share similar goals."

Photoshop (v.): for the purposes of this book, a strategy to improve your perception of life's more embarrassing moments

Plan B (n.): strategy that sane people use to keep from getting all wacked out over a single idea

playlist (n.): for the purposes of this book, your personal list of desired life experiences

pull a Wile E. Coyote (v.): get hit in the head by a boomerang you've "thrown" (see also *boomerang E-vite,* and *Focus Factor*)

RSVP (n.): what the Universe gives you in response to your E-vite; always *Yes*

snowball effect (n.): when good/bad energy attracts more of the same and things get better/worse quickly

thoughts to click send on (n.): ideas that put out the kind of energy that brings you what you want

V-card (n.): for the purposes of this book, the card you play every time you act like a victim

Victimville (n.): the place where you get stuck when you play the V-card too many times

Gratitudes

We really do keep a list of things we are grateful for. Here are some names that keep popping up.

To the girls who shared their stories with us and helped us see how much (and how little!) has changed since we were in high school—we thank them for their openness and for their most refreshing candor. A particular shout out to Gretel Dennis, who's living it up Down Under, for getting it right away and offering her ideas to us.

So many other people helped us to make this book happen. We thank Sangeeta Mehta, our editor at Simon & Schuster, for her enthusiasm and clear vision for what this book should be; Helen Brietweiser, our agent, who got us out there and kept us laughing the whole time; Dr. Linda Fallo-Mitchell and Theresa Joseph for opening the most important possible doors to love and understanding; Miriam Koller Pizzani, MD, for her psychiatric perspective and blessing of this work; Charlotte Tomaino, PhD, for her insight and interest in the power of the brain and the power of the mind; Eddy Yablans for going to bat for us; Joanne O'Sullivan for reviewing our proposal and giving us two thumbs-up; to Gina Legnani, "in angel" spelled backward, who was the first to say "it's fresh"; and to Elissa Hecker and Ken Swezey for their helpful advice.

You can't talk about teenagers without mentioning the cheerleaders. Our deepest thanks to those who cheered us on. Particular thanks to Valerie Henderson, who was the first kid on the block to know all this; Tara Turnbull and Elissa Patterson, who have a gift for balancing the spiritual with the practical; Amanda Creamer, who was there when it all went down; Kathy Murphy, for "airport time"; Eileen Baughan and Mary Thompson, rock stars and confidantes; Joany Lane, whose deep wisdom makes her the ultimate mother; Stefanie Wilson, a lifetime's greatest blessing; and Maria Guarnieri, because there are never enough chances to thank her.

To the girls we grew up with who saw us through the bad hair, the bad eyeliner, and the bad choices: We wouldn't change any of it. Those experiences are the foundation for this book, and those friendships are the foundation of who we are.

Above all, we are grateful to our families, who kept us grounded and inspired through the writing of this book. Thank you to the Monaghan Family; Tom, a perfect example of when the Universe delivers something better than you could have imagined; and Dain, Tommy, and Quinn, each a masterpiece in his own right.

And finally we'd like to thank the Wolfe Family: To Ed, for putting up with the piles of paper; and to Kole and Reese, whose realness, laughter, and inquisitiveness helped us remember who we really are deep down. We love you from the bottom of our hearts.

Sources

We referred to many articles and studies as we researched this book, including: Backster, C. "Evidence of a Primary Perception in Plant Life." *International Journal of Parapsychology*, 10(4), 1968: 329-48. The research of Aaron T. Beck, MD, Emmons, R. A. & McCullough, M. E. (2003). "Counting Blessings Versus Burdens: An Experimental Investigation of Gratitude and Subjective Well-Being in Daily Life." *Journal of Personality and Social Psychology* 84: 377-389. Emoto, M. *Hidden Messages in Water*. New York: Atria, 2005. Hagelin, J. S. et al (1999). "Results of the National Demonstration Project to Reduce Violent Crime and Improve Governmental Effectivenes in Washington D.C." *Social Indicators Research*, 47: 153-201. The work of Jerry and Esther Hicks, Nelson, R.D. et al. "Correlations of Continuous Random Data with Major World Events." *Foundations of Physics Letters*, 15(6), 2002: 537-550. The website http://noosphere.princeton.edu, which houses the documentation and serves as the communication interface for The Global Consciousness Project. Paivio, A. (1985). "Cognitive and motivational functions of imagery in human performance." *Canadian Journal of Applied Sport Sciences* 10: 22-28. Seligman, Martin E. P., PhD, *Authentic Happiness*, New York: Simon & Schuster, Inc. (2002). We are grateful to be among the beneficiaries of their work.

Notes